THE ART AND SCIENCE OF RESULTS

THE ART AND SCIENCE OF RESULTS

Dr. Joe Vitale

MEDIA

Published 2020 by Gildan Media LLC
aka G&D Media
www.GandDmedia.com

Front cover design by David Rheinhardt of Pyrographx

Interior design by Meghan Day Healey of Story Horse, LLC

Library of Congress Cataloging-in-Publication Data is available upon request

ISBN: 978-1-7225-0227-0

10   9   8   7   6   5   4   3   2   1

CONTENTS

CHAPTER SIX

The Third Clearing Technique:

CHAPTER SEVEN

The Fourth Clearing Technique:

CHAPTER EIGHT

The Fifth Clearing Technique:

CHAPTER NINE

The Sixth Clearing Technique:

CHAPTER TEN

The Seventh Clearing Technique:

CHAPTER ELEVEN

The Eighth Clearing Technique:

CHAPTER ONE

How to Get the Results You Want

'm an entrepreneur at heart; I'm a guy that's interested in results. I am interested in philosophy, I am interested in psychology, but if I can't take it to the bank, if I can't see actual concrete results, what's the point?

I've found that there are proven techniques to help people get the results that they've been dreaming about, striving for. I know what it's like to have sleepless nights wondering how you're going to pay bills. I know what it's like to go through the dark night of the soul. I know what it's like to be confused, to wonder, trying to figure out, how do I get results?

In this book I'm going to talk about the missing secret to getting results, and about a number of ways to get clear so you can get results. I'll even explain what I mean with concepts like *getting clear* and *results*. What do I mean by *beliefs*? What do I mean by *actions*, and which ones do you need to take and understand?

We have to look at science, where a scientist states a theory and then attempts to prove or disprove it. If they have proven it, they repeat it. If they're able to repeat it, other scientists will come in to test that theory by trying to repeat it as well. Science is trying to find the formulas, steps, procedures, and theories that actually work—in other words, the ones that get results. In this book I'll be looking at the science of getting results. Once I figured it out by testing it on myself, like a good scientist, I invite other people to test it on themselves. When we find it works, we will conclude that indeed there is a science to results, even though it hasn't been stated before.

We're talking about entrepreneurs who want to increase sales; artists who might want to sell their paintings or writings; somebody who wants to own a restaurant or open a new business. We're talking about people who might want a relationship when they haven't had one. They might want to go into fitness when they haven't been fit. We're talking about a wide range of results.

Consequently, we need flexibility within our formulas. That flexibility comes from personal creativity. I'm a big fan of stating an intention, but I'm also a big fan of allowing something greater than you to work. Call it your higher power; call it the creative aspect of your own mind;

call it the balance of the left and right brain. Call it all kind of things, but there's a system that can feed you new information that is outside the realm of current science.

This is where creativity, the art, comes in. For me, it's a blend of both. You want the science that gives you the guidelines. What is the formula? How do I achieve the result I want? But you also want the creativity, the art, the free-form improvisation that might give you a faster way to get results.

Science is always changing. You can go back through history and find out that science said that the earth was flat or that the sun went around the earth. New scientific discoveries have shown that some of the things that we thought were true aren't true. So the blend of science and creativity is where the real power is.

Even though life and technology are constantly changing, if you look back to earlier centuries, you'll find similar challenges. We still have the same desires. We want social approval; we want success, relationships, friendship. This will always be true in the human experience. We want the formulas, the science, and the tips for creating an art out of life. That's what I'm doing in this book—giving people tools that are useful today, but can still be useful in the next century, although it will have its own set of challenges.

I was born in Ohio into lower-middle-class family. My father worked on the railroad, raising four kids. My mother working at home, playing the traditional role of housewife. I wanted to be an author early on. When I was a teenager, I decided that I wanted to write books, plays, novels, but it took about three decades for my "overnight success" to come. During that struggle, I did go through homelessness. I did go through poverty. I was homeless in Dallas. In Houston I lived in poverty for over ten years.

Throughout it all, I had big dreams, big goals, big intentions. I thought I was doing everything correctly, and in many ways I was. I wasn't involved in self-destructive behavior. I wasn't drinking or doing drugs or gambling. I was doing all the right things, but I wasn't getting the right results.

So let me give you the first clue: I had to discover—with an earthshaking shock to my life—that my beliefs were creating my reality. This is something that I want you to soak up and chew on. I'll explain it and give the science behind it. Throughout this book, I'll talk about how to change your beliefs with different tools .

When I was living in Dallas, I was homeless. It was hell, because I didn't have a home. People used to ask, "What kind of car did you sleep in?" A car would have been great. I didn't have a car, so I slept on public benches outside the library, and during the day I was in the library. I lived and hid in the Dallas Public Library.

Thank goodness for the library. For a book addict like me, that is kind of heaven. Back then, the Dewey Decimal System said the 600 section was where psychology, philosophy, metaphysics, and success material were. I pretty much lived there, and as I kept reading all these books—*Think and Grow Rich, The Magic of Believing, How to Win Friends and Influence People,* the classics of success literature—over and over again, I saw that they talked about creating your own reality. Some of them were pretty blunt, saying that you create your own reality out of your beliefs. I heard this enough that I asked myself, "What kind of nutty beliefs would create homelessness?"

When I really dug deep, I found that there was a root core operating belief. Let me pause here to say that *every single one of us has a core operating belief.* We need to identify this and sometimes release and replace it to get the results we prefer.

In my case, when I looked at it deeply, I realized that I admired authors like Jack London, who wrote *The Call of the Wild, Martin Eden,* and *The Sea Wolf,* and Ernest Hemingway, who wrote *The Old Man and the Sea.* These guys were greats; their works are classics; we study them in school. They deeply influenced my writing style, but I mistakenly modeled my life on their lifestyles.

Jack London was alcoholic, suicidal, and dead by the age of forty. Ernest Hemingway struggled with alcoholism, violence, and mental illness, and died by his own hand. A part of me thought I had to go through that kind of drama in order to create a biography and earn a right to be successful.

A lot of people who are practicing the art of creativity— musicians, artists, painters—think they have to suffer before they can be successful. That's a belief. What I discovered is I was modeling myself after those authors because I thought I needed to have a sad life before I could have a successful one. That was my operating belief.

When I discovered it, and I was shocked by it. I had to say that surely there were authors out there who were prosperous, happy, healthy, and well-adjusted. Who were they? When I went looking, I found those people: the Ray Bradburys of the world and many other authors. When I got to meet them in later years and modeled their lifestyle, my life began to change. I started to get a different result.

So the lesson I want everybody to get from my life story is that when you change your beliefs, you get different results. That's a core message of this book.

Of course there are a number of people who, when they hear this, will start giving all sort of excuses, saying why this doesn't apply to them, why they have special circumstances that aren't letting them produce the results they want in life.

One is lack of education and training: "I didn't have the money to go to college. I made the mistake of not going to college." Or, "I'm in a field that dried up with the economy, and I'm forty-something years old. How am I going to get new training at this point?"

Another is lack of resources, usually money. People might say, "I've been wanting for years to start my own business. I have dreams of this; I invent things. Everyone else I know has gotten seed capital to start their business."

Still another thing might be not enough time: "I'd love to go off on my own and start my own enterprise, but I have such current work demands and income needs that I can't get out of this job cycle. I don't have enough time to give to these other dreams. I have family commitments; if I put too much time into my dreams, I'm going to neglect my family."

Another excuse might be lack of support from family or close relatives: "If I somehow become a success, I'll break away. I have an attachment to my family and my relatives, and I'll be separate from them in some way. Underneath it all, they may be kind of jealous, so I won't have that support system."

There's also discrimination. We hear a lot about that in society today: people feeling that because of their race, gender, or something else, they're being discriminated against and therefore they can't make it to the next level.

Finally, there's disability, which seems like a legitimate reason: "I'm disabled. I don't have legs, I can't see; I can't walk. How could I succeed?"

To all of these, I would kindly give a tough-love reply and say they're all nonsense. They are excuses. They are different forms of limiting beliefs. You can let them stop you, but if you really want results, you have to get past all of this.

Let's look at a couple of them. A lot of people use the excuse they don't have the money. I hear that all the time, but in reality, you don't need money. I wrote a book called *The Awakened Millionaire,* in which I pointed out what you need is creativity. There are many stories of people who have walked around the need for money by asking for it, by creating a crowd-funding resource, by doing any number of things to raise it, or by finding ways to create prototypes without using money at all.

There was a TV show on CNBC: Donny Deutsch's *The Big Idea.* I loved *The Big Idea.* At one point, he had a successful entrepreneur on, and he asked her, "How did you get started?"

"I had no education," she said. "I had no training. I had no money." She was a young, Afro-American woman, and she had an idea for an unusual purse. Now it seems to me that there are plenty of purses out there, so why create another one? But she did.

Then the woman thought, "How am I going to get this created with no money and no connections?" She Googled "purse manufacturers," and found that most of them were in China. She used her credit cards, got on a plane, and flew to China, although she didn't speak Chinese, didn't have a tour guide or a translator, and didn't have any contacts. She went to a hotel figuring that there'd be somebody there that could speak both English and Chinese.

The woman explained her situation. They gave her some numbers of purse manufacturers in the area. She contacted every one of them. One of them agreed to make a prototype on spec, so she came back to the United States with a couple of purses, which she was then able to shop. She found somebody who bought the purses, and then of course the rest is history. She's successful, and she's on Donny Deutsch's show talking about the big idea that was a big success.

This woman didn't need money. She didn't need training. She didn't need education. There was no discrimination. What she needed was courage, boldness, creativity, and taking action. And her results are stellar.

I was in the movie *The Secret*, and in it I said, "I'm going to get in your face, and I'm going to tell you the truth," and that's what I want to do in this book. It'd be the same thing if somebody came to me for mentoring or masterminding or personal coaching. I understand when somebody says, "I don't know where to start," or, "I don't know what to do," or, "I feel like I'm really limited," or, "I have these concerns and fears." I understand, because I've been there, but I also know that by using the principles I'm going to explain—the different ways to get clear— you can get past all that, you can take action, and you can get results.

Other internal impediments are preventing people from achieving the results they want in life. One of the biggest ones is fear. Fear of failure, fear of success, and even things like social anxiety. Some people have fear responses at a gut level, and they still have them no matter what they try to do to control their thoughts.

Another would be self-sabotage. In this case, a person starts on the right track. She goes over to China and gets the prototype, but then, for whatever reason, commits an act that totally sabotages her efforts. Or a player finally make it to the major leagues, faces his first major-league pitcher, and strikes out twelve times.

Then there are attitudinal problems: people are prone to having a negative attitude, to gossip, to be lazy while thinking, "I am working hard." You hear this a lot. Everybody feels they're working hard, but in reality, many people have an attitude of laziness. They're really not putting in the efforts required.

In response to all of this, I have good news. I've personally experienced most of these things firsthand (except maybe laziness). I understand the fear of failure, the fear of success, self-sabotage, not taking action. There are beliefs behind all of this. These behaviors are belief-driven, and I know how to remove and release them so I can get the results I want. In fact the clearing techniques that I'll be explaining are designed to help with these very issues.

You might be thinking, "That's not true at all. I really do want to take action. I believe I can take action." In this book you're going to discover the missing secret: we're not driven by what we consciously believe; we're driven by the beliefs that are in our subconscious/unconscious mind.

This hidden database usually doesn't come to the surface unless we do a little bit of exploring. It's not hiding; it's not under lock and key. We just have to turn a light on it. We're going to turn a light on it in this book. These techniques will help unearth and make visible some of those beliefs. Once you look at them, you can release them.

As for fear of failure, years ago, I met a billionaire years ago, a very famous, elderly man, and he said he had failed a lot. He'd gone bankrupt; he'd tried different ideas that didn't work. He said he learned something profound from failure: "Nothing bad happens to you. The world forgives, the world forgets. The only person that really hangs on is you, and if you can gain an insight and a lesson from it, there was never a failure to begin with."

Failure doesn't even have to exist. If you actually look at it as feedback, and you've renamed it and reframed it, then where's the failure? You learned something, and you can regroup, redirect, and move on.

Then there's the fear of success. Decades ago, I started to make a lot of money on the Internet, and then I hit a ceiling. I wondered, "How is this possible? There's nobody policing the Internet telling me, 'You've made too much money, so back off.'"

So the resistance had to be coming from me. I thought, "Am I self-sabotaging myself? Am I in some way, shape, or form tripping myself up from the results I wanted to get?" I looked really deeply, using some of the techniques that I'll describe, and I realized with a shudder that I didn't want to be more successful than my father.

I had to look at that and say, "I didn't even know it was there." This is what I mean by *hidden beliefs*. I didn't even know the belief was there until I had made a certain amount of money. I didn't want to make more than my father because I thought I might hurt his feelings, I might intimidate him, I might be boasting. So I had to question the belief, which is one thing I'll be discussing in this book.

When I questioned this belief, I realized, "Good Lord, my father wants me to be successful. He doesn't care if I make more money than him. He would be proud if I made more money than him, and he'd be astonished and interested and curious about how I was doing it." When I realized there wasn't anything to fear about success, and I could let that belief go, I was able to make more money. I got better results from looking at my beliefs.

The billionaire reframed failure as a result: "I just got a result." It might not be the one you want (and there's a system for getting the results that you want), but in the meantime, you can look at those failures simply as results. You can say, "I want to change those results," but without being weighed down with fear and regret.

Some people like to talk about missed opportunities. Many people feel that there's a window for producing results in a particular area and at some point that window closes. They think, "Yes, there's a window, and I have to cross that option off the list at a certain point in my life."

As a matter of fact, there *are* windows of opportunity, and guess what? There's one right now. There is a window of opportunity right now for you to step through, jump through, fly through. Entrepreneur Richard Branson said, "Opportunities are like buses. There's another one coming right around the corner."

Also, know that money likes speed; so does the universe, which means when you have an opportunity in front of you and the window is open, seize it. Grab it. Don't let it go.

Most of the other things are simply self-fulfilling prophecies. They are limiting beliefs that will come true as long as you believe them.

Once I went into a hotel gift shop, and there was an eighty-five-year-old woman working there. I was impressed because she was so upbeat and happy. She said it was *her* store. She wasn't just working it as a day job; she actually owned the store. I asked her how she did it, and she said, "I chose to."

"Well," I said, "everybody else about your age has decided they're going to go play with their grandkids."

"I've already played with grandkids," she said. "I want to do something with my life."

Then I asked, "What would you say to seniors came to you and asked for advice?"

"Anybody at any time can open their own business," she replied. "They can do whatever they want to do. There's nobody holding them back."

I get excited thinking that there are so many juicy opportunities. Yes, you might have passed up a few, but you're in this new moment: you're getting more aware, more excited, and more educated. You're learning different techniques to help you get results. When you jump through the window and go for the opportunity that's there, you've increased the likelihood that you're going to get the results that you actually want. The opportunity is right now.

At this point I suggest that you seize this moment and ask yourself, what do you want to have, do, or be? What's the result that you would like to have by the time you finish reading this book? Make a list. Go ahead, and say, "This is what I want to achieve. This is the result I want." Write that down so it's right in front of you.

This process is going to be wonderful, because as you go through this book, it will help your mind pick out all the nuggets that will help you achieve that result. Your result will also be in writing, so at the end of the book, you can go back and say, "Did I get that result or not?" If you write it down now, go through the steps, and do everything recommended, at the end of it you'll be able to cross that one off the list. You'll say, "OK, time for the next result."

Actually, it would be even juicer, more fun, and more energizing to write down ten or twenty or even 100 results. What would you really welcome in your life if you played with the possibility that knowing the art and the science and the techniques could make it happen?

CHAPTER TWO

You Must Clear a Path Before You Can Build a Road

As you're reading this, you may be excited by thinking of the results that you want from life. You may be saying, "Joe, I want to start building right now. Let's go ahead and start building towards those results."

We have to clear the path first. We have to clear the inner path before the outer path can lead to the result we want. The beliefs that we're holding are influencing the actions we're taking or not taking. So we have to go inside and look at our beliefs. We have to look at our programming.

If you're already in alignment with the result you want—which means that you don't have any limiting beliefs or excuses that are stopping you from taking action—then I say, "Go take your action steps. Go right to that program. Go right to that goal. Go ahead and start making it happen."

But if you run into a block or a snag or something seems to be turning into molasses in your approach, come back to this book, because my firsthand experience has been that virtually everybody has some limiting beliefs that are slowing down the process of getting the results they want.

Right now it's not so important right to be thinking, "What do I do on the outside?" You have to be looking at, "What do I do on the inside?"—meaning your internal mental programming. Align that, get clear of all the things that are in the way of making things happen, and then you can get the results you want.

I think this book is worth a million dollars. I think it's priceless, because I'm talking about a missing secret to success.

You have probably read self-help books, No doubt you know about material that's been out there for a couple of hundred years. Early books talked about having the life you want by believing in it, but you also know that not everybody gets the results that they want.

I was that way. I had to look in the mirror and ask, "Why am I doing the formula given by Napoleon Hill or Zig Ziglar or any of these other teachers, but I'm not getting the results they describe?"

At first there's frustration. Maybe you're throwing books against the wall. I did that too in the early days, saying, "Why am I not getting results? What's wrong with me?" Then you get to the big discovery: there's nothing wrong with you, but you have programming that you innocently inherited from other people as you were growing up. That programming is still active and operating today. Let me give you a couple of examples.

I wrote a book called *Attract Money Now*, and I teach people how to attract more money into their lives as entrepreneurs and as people who follow their passion.

You can consciously say, "This is the result I want. I want more sales for my business. I want to be on the Forbes 100 list." This is a positive goal; it is a noble intention.

However, if, in your deeper consciousness, in your subconscious/unconscious mind (I use these terms interchangeably), you have beliefs such as, "There's not enough to go around. Money corrupts. Money is bad. Money is evil. Only rich people get money, and they do it by criminal deeds. If I have a lot of money, the tax revenuers will come and take it; the corporations will take it. If I have a lot of money, my family and friends will abandon me. If I have a lot of money, I will lose my passion. I will lose my soul."

All of these are limiting beliefs. They are not facts. They are not truth. They are only true to the extent you believe in them. If people become entrepreneurs and take all the right action steps while these beliefs about money are hidden inside, they will not get the more money. They will innocently try all the right things. They will read all the right books. They'll do the formulas, but they will self-sabotage. They won't get the result they want, not because the formula is bad, but because their beliefs keep it from happening.

This is the missing secret. I believe if I have any I have made any contribution in all of my work, it's this idea that until you get clear of the limiting beliefs in your unconscious/subconscious mind, you are either going to delay, stop, stall, or be unable to hold on to the result you actually want.

You must get clear. What are you getting clear of? Your beliefs.

A lot of times people say, "I agree with you, Joe, that this is a limiting belief, but somehow it just keeps popping up automatically, and I cannot shut it off."

Say you were raised from a very young age in an extremely dysfunctional family, which reinforced these muddled beliefs. Then there's someone who has been abused physically, sexually, or otherwise. There's trauma from accidents or fighting overseas, or catastrophic failures involving public humiliation. There's also societal programming and peer influence, telling us that this is just the way things are. Media and social media constantly reinforce the victimhood mentality.

The good news is all of this can be healed; all of this can be cleared and overcome so that you can start to get the results you want. You can heal your wounds.

The mass of people are struggling, they're desperate, and they feel like victims. I certainly remember that from being homeless and in poverty. I felt like a victim. I felt that the world was against me.

I have a mission—to make victimhood optional. The techniques in this book are designed to clear the debris of virtually anything you can mention. Even childhood programming, trauma, massive failures, and societal programming can be handled with these techniques.

You were innocently programmed. It is not your fault that you got the programming that you got, but it *is* your responsibility. There's no blame, no guilt. This happens to be what you've inherited. This is what you have at this point. I'm going to give you a number of techniques that will help you get clear of this unfortunate inheritance.

Where do limiting beliefs come from? Some are in the culture itself; some are in the religion we grew up in; some are in the educational system. In the household that we were born and raised in, before the age of five, we downloaded a lot of information from our family, neighbors, and others.

I ask people, "Were your parents Mr. and Mrs. Buddha?" They laugh and say, "No." Our parents had their own programming, they had their own limitations, and they were innocently programmed as well. At whatever age you are, you have your bag of beliefs, but the good news is you can be free of it. I have seen people go from hopelessness to abundance by learning how to use these clearing techniques. By using them, I've completely rewired my own brain and play with possibilities for even bigger expansion.

I smile when I start to think about all the possibilities that you can have when you do the work inside. That's the missing secret. Deal with the beliefs that you inherited, then, as you take action, you can get the results that you want.

You might be asking how long it takes to clear away the debris of these undesirable beliefs. I love that question, because it reveals an opportunity to look at a belief right now. The answer depends on what you believe. Maybe you believe, "I've had this luggage for three decades, and it was anchored in when I was five years old, so this is not going to be removed overnight through some book by Joe Vitale. It's going to take some doing. I need to see a therapist; I need to have magic mojo sprinkled on me." If so, you will be creating a belief that will make it a requirement to take longer.

On the other side, if you have a belief that you can change with the right tip, the right technique, the right story, the right inspiration, the right moment, the right person, then you can do it in an instant.

How long does it take? As long as you believe.

I'm a hypnotist, and I've been into hypnosis since the 1960s. When I was a kid I was fascinated by it. I'm not talking about hypnosis for the stage or entertainment. I'm talking about counseling hypnosis.

When we speak to the unconscious mind and give it a new story, it can wipe out the old story and the paradigm and beliefs that were behind it. You're still you, but now the blocks and limitations and barriers have dropped away. Why? Because you have a new reality. That new reality is based on a story.

How long does it take? How long do you believe it'll take? It could happen while you're reading this chapter. It could happen with any one of the techniques we'll be going through. It can happen tonight when you go to sleep. You've been reading this book, and the ideas in it have been incubating inside your soul. You could go to sleep tonight, have a dream, and in that dream realize, "Wow! I can hand back all the beliefs that were given to me!" and you can awaken in the morning free of them. It all happened in a dream. It can be that easy.

One big tip: *we usually are not aware of our limiting beliefs.* This is why reading a book like this is so useful. It will become a mirror for you. As you read about stories, processes, and techniques, you'll have little aha! experiences and realize, "Oh, I didn't even know that was a limiting belief." Now you do.

One time I had lunch with a friend, and she said, "Affirmations don't work for me." (Affirmations are statements of positive intent to reprogram your mind.)

I looked at her, and I said, "Do you know that's an affirmation?"

She was saying, "Affirmations don't work for me" as an unconscious affirmation. This is why we need coaching, mentoring, and books like this—to become aware of our beliefs. At that point we can look at them and question them, and then that belief is gone.

While you're reading this, think of your current concern or problem and the result that you want to have. You can read this book with an eye towards what can be of service to you in regard to this issue. Anybody going through a problem or a challenge right now should be asking, "How can this material help me?" Pay attention to the key, the phrase, the story, the technique that you can apply to get the result that you want.

One basic idea is the four stages of awakening. This helped make sense of all the confusing and conflicting psychology, philosophy, metaphysics, and models of the world. I would look at them and go, "How can this particular way of living exist, and this other one, which looks like the direct opposite, exist in the same world? How is this possible?"

I've learned that there are stages of consciousness, what I've called the four stages of awakening. The first one is *victimhood*. Henry David Thoreau said, "The vast majority of men lead lives of quiet desperation." (Of course, today you'd say men and women and children lead lives of quiet desperation.)

At this stage, people feel like victims. They feel they're alone. They feel they don't have any power. They don't have the skills or techniques to get the results they want, so in many ways, they're zombies. They're the walking dead. I've been there and I know what that is like.

The second stage is *empowerment*. Empowerment is when you begin to realize you have more power than you ever thought. You start to feel like a young Superman or Superwoman, and you start to learn the techniques that will help you get the results you want. You start to visualize, you start to affirm, you start to take action, and you start to get more positive results. It is a powerful, thrilling stage to be in. I want everybody to be in the empowerment stage, because it's much better than rolling over and playing dead as a victim.

Those are the first two stages, but there are two more, and they're better than empowerment. Given the way I just described empowerment, those other two stages must be off-the-charts wonderful. In chapter 13, I will reveal those stages. They're particularly powerful because they take us beyond mere beliefs into a deeper experience of your spiritual understanding of your life.

To wrap up this chapter, we can ask, what are some steps you can take to determine which stage you're in? Sometimes we like to fool ourselves. We think that we're really in stage two when we might be in stage one in certain areas.

The easiest way of determining the stage you're in is to ask, whom are you blaming? If you're blaming anybody else, if you're looking out there and saying, "It's the government, it's the terrorists, it's my family, it's my neighbors, it's my boss, it's the economy," you're making a statement of victimhood.

If you are taking responsibility—not blaming yourself but saying, "I've created my reality, and I'm going to create it differently because I'm learning how to create new results"—you are moving into empowerment.

It's wise to look at different categories of life, because maybe in business you're feeling more empowered, while in your personal relationships you're feeling more like a victim. We want to move all of these areas into empowerment. Later we can move them further up the ladder, but we certainly don't want to be in victimhood.

Victimhood is not a place that is happy. It is not a place that is healthy. It is not a place that is creative. It is not a place that is light; it comes more from the dark. It is not a place where you can really live, because in a sense it's more of a dying.

Be aware of where you are. Are you blaming anybody else? If so, you're probably in victimhood. Are you taking responsibility for your life and doing things to move forward? Then you're in empowerment. That's where I would begin.

CHAPTER THREE

The Life-Changing Impact of Your Beliefs

We've discussed beliefs already, but let's dig a bit deeper to really crystalize exactly what a belief is and how it is distinguished from other things that people might think are beliefs.

To start with, let's look at the difference between belief and faith. If someone says, "I have religious faith. I have faith in the leadership we have in this country," is that the same or different from belief?

Quite a few years ago, I wrote a book called *Faith*, in which I said there were three kinds of faith: faith in yourself; faith in the world, which means other people; and faith in what we'll call a higher power. All three of these are belief-based. Faith is having a belief in yourself, other people, or a higher power, so it is very much belief-based. Both beliefs and faith are choice-based. So if you want to have more faith in yourself, actually at heart it's a choice.

Let's go deeper. If somebody doesn't choose to believe in themselves or in other people or in a higher power, there's still a belief behind that. This is why it's so crucial to grasp that we are operating from beliefs. We don't realize this, because the beliefs are subconscious/ unconscious. We need to bring them to the surface so we can question them.

If somebody says, "I don't have faith in myself," why not? They have beliefs about themselves, most likely based on past experience. Maybe they tried something, and it didn't work out the way they wanted, so they concluded they weren't good enough; they didn't know what they were doing; they didn't have enough education.

All of these conclusion are beliefs. This is why it is so important to explore beliefs. *We live in a belief-driven universe.* If you change your beliefs, you get a different universe. Another way to say it is if you change your beliefs, you get different results.

There is a clear difference between beliefs and facts, and this is very useful for us. If you're starting to wonder what a belief is and what your own beliefs are, you have to look at the difference between a belief and a fact.

For example, there's a yellow pencil right here on the table in front of me. I'm picking it up, and I could say that yellow pencils bring me luck. When I look at a yellow pencil, to me it means good luck.

When you look at a yellow pencil, what do you see? Probably a writing device, something you can draw with. It's a yellow number 2 pencil with a piece of graphite in it and an eraser on the end. That is a fact. But for me, it's lucky. That's a belief. Somebody else may see a pencil as a weapon: you can use it for self-defense. You could use it as a dart, so it could be for sport.

We can agree about the fact that this object is a pencil. But when I say, "Pencils are lucky," that would be a belief about it.

It's a little bit like somebody who says, "I only wear purple shirts when I speak, because I give my best speeches when I wear a purple shirt." That is a belief about purple shirts. That the shirt is purple is a fact. You look at it, and most of us are going to agree about its color. The emotion you project onto that fact by saying, "This purple shirt empowers me as a speaker"—that's a belief.

It's the same thing when somebody says money is bad. Is this a fact or a belief?

Money is just paper and coin, an agreed-upon means of exchange. It's not good or bad in and of itself. It's neutral. When somebody says money is bad, that's a belief. It's not a fact.

Usually a fact is something that is measurable, and we can all agree on it. We can all agree on the external characteristics of a pencil—it's yellow, it's so many inches long, and so on—but if I say pencils are lucky, we won't all agree on that. That indicates that it must be a belief, not a fact.

We can ask, "Does everybody agree on this?" If everybody agrees, it's in the direction of a fact. If there is argument, if there is confusion, if there is questioning or all sides, we'd say that's probably in the nature of a belief. Then we need to ask, which of my beliefs are serving me now and will serve me to get the result I want?

If somebody says, "I want to be an entrepreneur and be independently wealthy, but the current economy makes it difficult," would we all agree on that? I don't think so. Many people would, which means that there is an audience that would be supportive of your limiting belief. At the same time, other people, such as Richard Branson and Bill Gates, are doing big, daring, exciting things and would say, "Now is the greatest opportunity of all time to be an entrepreneur. There is no limitation out there."

As I've said, we live in a belief-driven universe; therefore life is an optical illusion. You see whatever you believe. If somebody is saying, "I want to be an entrepreneur, but . . ." what they are saying about the situation is based on their beliefs. When they look out into the universe, they look into the world of possibilities. When they read the newspaper or look on the Internet, they're going to see a match to their beliefs. When they see that match, they'll say, "See? Told you so."

Here's the punch line. If you change your inner beliefs, you change your perceptions and your mind-set. You look out onto the same universe, but now it's presenting things that match your new beliefs.

How does this happen? Science says there are mirror neurons in our brain, which find matches to what we're already thinking. Carl Jung and other great psychologists also said that what is out there is a mirror reflection of what is inside of you. If you change the inside of you, you get a different reflection back.

I like saying life is an optical illusion because it helps explain why so many people can have beliefs that oppose each other while still being in the same universe. They're selectively seeing a match to their beliefs.

Let's bring all of this back home to results. "I'm not getting the results I want," or, "I am getting the results I want." Those statements are based on a set of beliefs that are already in place. This set of beliefs is called a *paradigm*.

In this book, I'll be exposing your paradigm, so you can find out what's operating to get you the results you currently have. If you don't like the paradigm or you don't like your results, you can change them. You can install new beliefs; then you'll start to get the results you prefer.

I have a concept that I call the *three-day rule*. In general, it says that what you're seeing and what you're feeling right now will generally happen in about three days.

But this doesn't always happen. Why? Because you have beliefs that counter it or slow it down from taking place. If you state something, visualize it, repeat it, and put some emotion into it, it will generally come about in three days unless you are also doing the opposite and focusing on something else that you don't want.

What's going on here scientifically? Your reticular activating system has been engaged. The reticular activating system is at the base of the brain, at the top of the spine. It's already programmed for survival. So congratulations: your reticular activating system is working: you are alive. But most people don't know that you can program it for something more than survival. You can program it to get a result that you want.

This reticular activating system responds to *imagery*, *emotion*, and *repetition*. So you have to visualize the result you want. What does it look like? Is it a car? Is it a business? Is it a relationship? Create some sort of image or graphic representation of it. You want an image of the result that you want. That's the target.

The second thing you need to have for the reticular activating system is emotion. We do not create without emotion. Unfortunately, most people are focused on what they hate or what they fear. Fear and hate dominate their minds, so that's what they end up looking for and attracting, I want you to focus on what you love. What do you want? What are you passionate about? What excites you? That positive emotion. So you have an image of the results you want. Now you have a positive emotion, love, for these results.

The third step is repetition. This is why people do vision boards. They have a wall or a mirror or an image on their computer that shows a picture of what they want. You look at it repeatedly and with emotion, because you're programming the reticular activating system to say, "I want this result." Almost magically, the subconscious/ unconscious mind will maneuver your way in life to make that result happen.

*   *   *

Throughout this book, I'll be giving nine main techniques for clearing your mind and redesigning your beliefs for optimal results. I would recommend that you go through these in the order in which they're presented. That will give you have a base understanding of what each one does and how they work.

After that, you can then say, "I really like technique three or technique seven, or I really like two through five." You can pick and choose what you want. Treat this book as a buffet of clearing techniques. After you walk up and down the line, and you see what is there, and maybe take a little sample of each one, then you can say, "I really like that second one. I'm going to go back to that." Use the one that most appeals to you.

Now I don't want to inhibit anybody. If you have the creative impulse to jump to something that sounds interesting, Godspeed to you. Jump there, soak it up, and practice it. Then at some point come back and go through the rest of the techniques, because, like a good buffet, this book might have some yummy stuff that you walked by the first time.

Some people have asked me what beliefs are most in line with peak performance. I think the smartest thing to do is to give you a simple assignment, because, after working with hundreds of people, I've found that when you state the result that you want, the limiting beliefs in the way of achieving it start to bubble to the surface.

So do this: state your intention. What do you want the result to be? Write it down. You can do it on your phone, you can do it anywhere, but by doing it with a piece of paper and a pen, you can actually see it and feel it, because you're writing with your hand.

Write down, "This is the result that I want. I intend to achieve—" Write it down. Think big. Think clearly. Think daringly. Don't be inhibited. Think without any restrictions. Do your best to just lay it on the line.

Pretend that you went to someone who could grant you one of your greatest wishes. What would that be? Write it down.

Then sit with your desired result for a moment and say, "What does it feel like?" What do you feel about that result? What comes up for you? What would be stopping you from achieving it? Whatever those thoughts are, write those down, because they are going to be a clue to the beliefs that have been stopping you.

This is a very powerful, revelatory technique, and it's so easy to do. I'm probably going to do it myself right after this, because it's so useful to unearth any limiting beliefs that keep surfacing.

So you write down your intention. What is your goal? What is your desired result? Be as clear as you possibly can. Be honest with yourself. Don't pull back. Say, "This is the result I want."

Then the second step is to look at it, feel it, and imagine it. What comes to mind? What bubbles up from the surface that could be a limiting belief? "I'm too old, I'm too young, I'm too fat, I'm too thin, I don't have the resources, I don't have the money, I don't have the connections, I don't know where to start." There are a billion things that could come up, but whatever it is for you, write them down.

Then, as we go through the rest of this book, we will knock out these limiting beliefs. As we do, it's going to be easier for you to achieve your intended result.

CHAPTER FOUR

The First
Clearing Technique:
Socratic Questioning

et's begin by sorting through some misconceptions about clearing techniques. To many people, using a technique to clear our consciousness might seem too simplistic. Psychology and psychiatry often tell us that some people have built up beliefs and attitudes about life that may take years to effectively change because deep-seated psychological conditions, childhood imprinting, and trauma. Neuroscience is also showing strong genetic predispositions to being positive or more melancholy.

As a matter of fact, I have a lot of scientific information that proves that we live in an unlimited universe. It's not true that you are destined to live with what you have. Neuroscience is proving with case study after case study that it doesn't matter what you start with. People are rewiring their brains.

Brain scientist Jill Bolte Taylor wrote a book called *My Stroke of Genius*. She'd had a stroke, and she couldn't use part of the left side of her brain, so she learned how to do everything with the other part. Earlier scientists said that was impossible, that if you lost the use of one part of your brain, you can't replace it with the other half. We found out that's not true.

Biologist Bruce Lipton wrote a book called *The Biology of Belief*, in which he showed that because of epigenetics, you can turn your DNA on and off with your beliefs. This is telling people, "Look, you can't come up with these excuses anymore. Yes, you might have had some struggle growing up, some abuse, or something you inherited, but that doesn't have to stop you. You can regroup, you can refocus."

Then, there's Dr. Joe Dispenza, who wrote a book called *You Are the Placebo*. It points out that what you believe becomes your reality. Other people can say, "That medicine's not really real. It's just a placebo," but it works all the same. What you believe is real.

Science is drowning us with the idea that you can have, do, or be anything you want. The only limitation comes from yourself, from your own idea of what you think is possible. Guess what? What you think is possible is also a belief.

Another book, by Jeffrey Schwartz, is *You Are Not Your Brain.* Scientific proof indicates that you are almost separate from your brain and your body. You have an almost mystical, superhuman power, and you use it when you start to believe that it exists for you.

That's why I'm so excited. Every one of these clearing techniques empowers you to get the result that you've written down.

The first technique is *Socratic questioning.* It goes back to Socrates, a Greek philosopher of the fifth century BC, who used this technique to help people to reach insights, but there also have been a lot of Socratic teachers down the road.

Barry Neil Kaufman wrote a book called *To Love Is to Be Happy With.* He had a child that was born autistic, and he tried to have his child cured through the scientific means that were available at the time. The experts said, "You have other kids. This one's the throwaway. You can't really do anything with this."

Barry didn't accept this verdict. At that point he started questioning the scientific community, and he started questioning the beliefs around autism in general. He developed his own way of working with his child, and in seven years, that child was diagnosed as no longer autistic. He's a full-grown adult at this point. Barry wrote a book about his experience called *Sunrise*;

there was also a movie made about it with the same title.

Kaufman developed a technique that he learned from Bruce Di Marsico, which had to do with questioning beliefs. I started to research the subject, and there was another teacher, the late Morty Lefkoe, whom I worked with closely and whom I greatly miss even today. He had developed another clearing technique, which was a specific way of questioning beliefs. Then I looked even deeper into the metaphysical literature, such as Jane Roberts and the Seth material. That was all about questioning beliefs.

I then started turning the X-ray machine on my own brain to find out what my beliefs were and to question and change them. I coined the phrase *Socratic questioning technique*. Basically it consists of a few questions that you can ask yourself about any particular belief.

This is internal work. I usually tell people to write the questions out, because when we try to do a dialogue around questions in our mind, we run in circles. We don't usually see our thoughts because we're thinking them. We don't usually question our beliefs because our beliefs seem like reality to us. We don't question these things because it doesn't even occur to us to question them.

Let's go back to where we were in the previous chapter, where I said to write down the result you want and pay attention to the beliefs that surface as a result.

Now you have a list of potential limiting beliefs. What do you do with it? Question them. How do you question them? We can make it really simple: just ask, is it a belief or a fact?

I can give you a more scientific formula for questioning those beliefs. Write the belief down in front of you. It could be things like, "There isn't enough time." "I don't have enough money." "I don't know how to make the first step." "I don't feel I'm good enough." "I don't feel I'm smart enough." Reach out to come up with other beliefs. What came to mind? Pick one of them. Then ask, "What do I believe about this belief?" Write down whatever comes to mind.

The second question is, "Why do I believe it?" This is an important one. You're looking for your own evidence for your belief. Where did it come from? Why do you believe your belief? Pretend you are an attorney: you are trying the case of this belief, and you are asking, "Where is the evidence for this?"

Several years ago, when I was about to turn sixty, I decided that I wanted to be a musician. It was on my bucket list. I wanted to go in the studio and record, but I had never done it before.

All my limiting beliefs came up. "I don't have any talent." "I don't know how to sing. I don't even sing in the shower." "I don't know how to write songs." I had a guitar but only knew three chords. "I don't know anything. I don't know how to work with a band. I don't know how to be in a music studio."

I took a songwriting class with Ray Wylie Hubbard and Kevin Welch, two well-known singers of Americana. Ray Wylie Hubbard said something fascinating: he still had limiting beliefs come up for him whenever he tried something new. So I don't think it's unusual for people to have limiting beliefs. They will come up whenever we try for something we've never done before. So be easy with yourself. We all have limiting beliefs. Me too.

Ray Wylie Hubbard said that these beliefs would come up, but then he asked an important question: where's the evidence that I *can't* do this?

It was life-changing for me, because I thought, "There isn't any evidence." Although I had beliefs about becoming a musician and a singer/songwriter and was terrified by the idea of being on stage, I couldn't find any evidence that supported these beliefs. There was no evidence that I couldn't do it. I could say I hadn't done it yet, but there wasn't anything that said I *couldn't* do it.

That's what you're looking for: Why do I believe this? What's the evidence for this particular belief? More often than not, when you start looking, you won't find any evidence, and then that belief will weaken. It can even leave; it can be erased; it can melt, because there's no evidence for it. It's almost like a ghost. When you asked, "Where's the ghost?" and you looked, it disappeared. It was just a whisper.

But say that you do have some evidence. When I was growing up, my father said, "The best way to double your money is to fold it over and put it back in your pocket." It wasn't until decades later that I thought, "What a limiting belief that was!" but I didn't know it at the time. It was my authority figure, my father, telling me in his wisdom from life, "Here's the way to make money. Fold it over, and put it back in your pocket."

For decades, I didn't have money; I was struggling; I went through homelessness. Finally I started to question my beliefs about money. For one, that it's scarce. Why do I believe it's scarce? I heard from my father that it was scarce. Where's the evidence that that's actually true? There isn't any. There are plenty of people out there who spend their money, invest their money, give their money, and more money comes back to them.

Again, with this step-by-step system I'm encouraging you to question your beliefs. The first question is, what do I believe about that belief? The second one is, why do I believe it?

The third question is, why do I believe the evidence for it? The fourth is, what would be better to believe than that belief? That's a biggie, because in some situations, you will erase a belief and it will be gone. In other situations, you might want to replace the belief.

My father said things like, "Fold your money over" or, "Money doesn't grow on trees"—things we've all heard. But we don't understand that these beliefs lodge in our consciousness; they become part of our perception, and then part of our mental programming and paradigm. When we look out at the optical illusion of life, we see a match to our limiting beliefs about money. Most of the time we're operating from hidden, unconscious/subconscious beliefs, so we're bumbling through life because we haven't stopped to look.

So when we get to the point where we've questioned the belief, and we see that there's no real evidence for it, we can say, "What would be better to believe?"

At one point I decided to take on a new belief: "The more money I spend, the more money I receive." When I first stated it, I thought, "That's a pretty bold belief." Surely a CPA and the IRS would say, "No, that's wrong. The more money you spend, the less money you have. You've lost."

But I took on my new belief. At first it was uncomfortable, because I felt I was lying to myself. And some people think that when they take on a new belief, they are lying to themselves. Actually, you're creating a new mind map. You're creating new neural pathways in your brain.

When you first state the new belief, it is uncomfortable, and it does feel unreal, because at that point it still is. But as you keep saying it, you keep living it, and you engage the reticular activating system with imagery, emotion, and repetition. Before you know it, this becomes a new belief.

Guess what? Today the more money I spend, the more money I receive. It's my new reality. That's the power of this scientific formula, which uses the Socratic questioning technique on belief. Look at the belief, question it, and look for the evidence for it. Once you've weakened and then dismantled it, you can ask, what would be better to believe? and you can choose a different belief.

The meaning you give an event is the belief that actually created the event. Everything that's happening to you in your life, the results or lack of results that you're getting, are stemming from these unconscious beliefs.

One way to find out the unconscious belief is to look at the meaning you gave the event. How do you do that?

Go have coffee or a beer or wine with a friend of yours, and tell them what happened: "I tried to open my business, or I tried to go on this date, and here's what took place." You're listening for the *turning-point belief.* You will state it as if it's reality.

A woman who's been trying to go on dates but hasn't have them work out might say, "I've been on date after date. I went to a dating site, and I went to a social group. I've met person after person, but they're not working out." Then she says, "All the good ones are taken."

That was the belief that created the experience she is now describing. She created a self-fulfilling prophecy. She created a situation of not finding the right person because she had a prior belief that all the good ones are taken. She might be saying, "I've accumulated evidence, and therefore I'm justified in this belief," but in reality the belief enabled her to gather the evidence.

This insight alone is worth the price of this book, because somebody who grasps and integrates it will start to look at life differently. To the person who said, "All the good ones are taken," I can reply, "There are over seven billion people on the planet. Does it seem reasonable that all the good ones are taken?" This can start to dislodge the belief. The person can go through the questioning process and realize, "That belief isn't really serving me, and it is not a fact." It's not a fact. It's your opinion. Your opinion is your belief.

It's the same thing if somebody says, "I opened three different coffee shops, and it didn't work out. There's so much competition out there that there's no way that another coffee shop is going to make it." That's their story; that's their insight. They should stop and realize that the meaning they gave the event is the belief that created it. Their conclusion was actually the belief that caused the event in the first place.

Unconsciously, this person was thinking, "Coffee shops aren't going to work out, because there's so much competition." Then consciously they start a coffee shop, because they're not aware of the unconscious belief. When it doesn't work out, they spout the unconscious belief.

Recently I was in Italy. I drank a lot of coffee and saw lots of coffee shops. It is amazing how many coffee shops, all independent, are on every corner and how many times a day people drink coffee. In my opinion, there are abundant opportunities for people to open coffee shops. So my experience and belief are completely different from that of the person who says, "I tried three different locations. They didn't work out. Too much competition."

In this process, it's important to do no harm and stay nonjudgmental. Your main goal here is not to aim weapons but to shine a light. When we say, "All the good ones are taken," or, "I've opened three coffee shops that haven't worked out," we can start to beat ourselves up: "What's wrong with me? I've questioned my beliefs. I'm doing the things, and it's still not working out."

Love yourself. Forgive yourself. Appreciate yourself. Be kind to yourself. Be gentle with yourself. It is a scientific fact that self-punishment does not help you. A lot of people might use the psychological whipping technique, thinking that they have to feel guilty to motivate themselves to go to the gym, for example. Research and science have shown that that is very short-lived. If you're motivated by the negative, you're not going to enjoy the process, so you're going to give it up very quickly. Then you'll probably punish yourself for stopping.

Positive psychology is a more beneficial approach. With positive psychology, which is scientifically based, you focus on what's working. You focus on what's positive. You focus on what's good. You focus on what's healthy. You focus on what you're doing right, because that awareness will expand, and you'll do more of what's right. Self-punishment is not going to help. Self-appreciation will build your self-esteem. It will build your muscle of confidence, and you'll be able to get more of the results you want.

When I was homeless, my self-esteem and self-confidence were zero, so it was almost impossible to achieve any results. I was a solitary man trying to make some difference in my life, so it took forever to build these traits up in me. The good news for you is that you can do it right now. The fact that you've invested in yourself by reading this book is a value you want to reinforce and acknowledge. You *are* taking care of yourself. You *do* care about yourself. You *are* worth it. That's the mentality we want to have.

Some people may be wondering whether they should do Socratic questioning with a partner: should I have someone ask me these questions, to which I respond, or should I do it on my own?

First of all, everything I'm describing here is designed to be done independently, so you can do it on your own. Nevertheless, I know from firsthand experience that if you use this Socratic questioning method with somebody else, it'll be more powerful, and usually the results will be accelerated, because the other person is obviously outside of you. They don't have the same beliefs you do. There may be some overlap, but if you're with a skilled person who can listen, who can reflect back to you what you're saying, who can ask the questions with a sense of neutrality and acceptance, without attachment or judgment, it can help you see what your own beliefs are.

When you explore beliefs on your own, there is a tendency to think, "It's reality." You believe it to be that way because it's been your life experience, whereas another person can question your beliefs. When they do, maybe for the first time, you realize, "That was a belief. I was thinking it was a fact."

To repeat: there's no judgment in this process, no negativity. Pretend you're a happy detective looking for clues to beliefs.

About fifteen years ago, I met a young man in Thailand. He was twenty years old, and he was homeless. He was sleeping on the beaches outside of Bangkok, and he had nothing and no one and no money. No car to sleep in. He was desperate.

He had reached out to a friend from his native country, which was Sweden, and asked for money, but the friend said, "I'm not going to send you any money, but I'll send you a book."

The friend sent *The Secret*. Later it was turned into a movie, and if you haven't read the book or seen the movie, you should. It's an inspiring story about the law of attraction.

My homeless friend was upset at first: "Why in the world am I being sent this? I am starving. I don't need a book." But he started to read it, and he was fascinated by the concepts of looking at and changing your beliefs, visualization, affirmation, goal setting, and faith in yourself, other people, and the world at large.

My friend decided to prove it all wrong. He decided to prove that he *couldn't* get results with this methodology. He did all the techniques: he started using affirmations; he started writing down and questioning his beliefs. He got more interested, and he read my books, Bob Proctor's, Jack Canfield's, as well as some of the other authors that are out there.

Now, years later, at the age of thirty-six, he is a billionaire. He's the largest real-estate developer in southern Thailand. My friend told me that he did the belief work. He was looking at beliefs like, "I am homeless." He wondered, "How can I get a meal with an affirmation or a visualization or a clearing technique?" But over time, he kept getting what he wanted, manifesting it, attracting it. He kept going for even bigger and better things, opening different businesses. Now he has twenty businesses with 200 employees.

I told him he needed to write his life story, and I wisely said he should hire me to do it. He did hire me, and we did write it, and that book is out. It's called *Homeless to Billionaire: The 18 Secrets to Attracting Great Wealth and Seeing Great Opportunity*. His name is Andres Pira.

CHAPTER FIVE

The Second Clearing Technique: Ho'oponopono

f you're reading about this for the first time, buckle up; fasten your seat belts. This is mind-blowing. It was for me, and it has been for everybody since, because I've written about the story in two different books, *Zero Limits*, and later in *At Zero*.

Way back, I was in New Hampshire at a National Guild of Hypnotists convention, where I was one of the speakers. During a break, somebody asked me, "Hey, did you ever hear about that therapist who helped heal an entire ward of mentally ill criminals in the state hospital in Hawaii?"

"No," I said, "I never heard of that."

"It's fascinating, because he didn't actually work with the patients. He worked on himself using some weird Hawaiian technique, and they got better."

"I'm pretty open-minded," I thought. "I'm interested in magic and miracles, but this sounds like an urban legend." Curing incurably insane criminals? It just didn't sound believable. So I dismissed it. It shows you how open-minded I was.

A year later, I heard the story again. At that point I started doing some research.

Back then, there was very little information about this man. There were no books out there on him or his technique, but I can be persistent, and I found him. His name was Dr. Ihaleakala Hew Len. He was the therapist at the hospital for the criminally insane in Hawaii.

I found him and got him on the phone. He explained that yes, he worked for four years at that state hospital, and yes, he used an unusual Hawaiian technique, and yes, it was based on clearing his beliefs. As he cleared his beliefs, those patients got better.

That just sounds preposterous. How is that possible? How could this work?

Nevertheless, this particular technique is worth millions in terms of pain release, healing, breakthroughs, and getting results. It has been proven the world over and over again. There are scientific studies behind it. People have analyzed it to find out what's going on.

I interviewed Dr. Hew Len, and I ended up doing a workshop with him. I talked him into coauthoring the first book, which is called *Zero Limits*, which has caused a whole movement of people to find out more about this technique. We've done three seminars together. We called them "Zero Limits 1, 2, and 3." They are all based on a technique called *ho'oponopono* in the Hawaiian language.

Basically, ho'oponopono assumes that there is no real *outer* in the world. It is all an inside job. Everything you see on the outer—where do you see it? You see it in your mind. Where is your mind? Inside you.

So if you look out and see a problem, or you see somebody that's bothering you, that's actually like watching a film. Where is the film being projected from? Inside the projector. Where's the projector? Inside of you.

When you're looking at things from the ho'oponopono perspective, you remember that everything you're seeing on the outside is a reflection of what's inside you. So if you want to change, you have to do it inside you. Trying to change the outer is like standing in front of a mirror to shave but shaving the mirror.

In reality, that's what most of us are doing. We're messing with the outer world, when we need to work with our *inner* beliefs on the *inner* world. So one of the first premises is that *the world is a mirror.*

The next one is that *you take 100 percent responsibility for your life.* That is something bigger than most people have ever heard of. When I first met Dr. Hew Len, he said, "Have you ever heard the concept you create your own reality?"

"Sure," I said. "I'm one of the authors who write about it and talk about it."

"Well, if you create your own reality and a mentally ill criminal is in your reality, didn't you create that person too?"

It was a mind stopper, because I started to look at the people or relationships that were bothering me at the time, as well as the results I was getting or not getting. I had to realize, "This is all me. This is all coming from me. All the results, or lack of results, I am 100 percent responsible for."

Now let me remind you of a point I made earlier: you are not to blame. It's not your fault that you have something to deal with, but it *is* your responsibility to deal with it.

In this case, Dr. Hew Len was teaching me, "You're 100 percent responsible." This is a quantum leap in responsibility. When I first heard it, it pulled my brain like taffy.

Most people look at "you create your own reality" from the perspective that you're responsible for what you say and do, but in ho'oponopono, you're responsible for *everything* and *everybody*. This is huge.

The third thing that Dr. Hew Len taught was that *everything is occurring in your life because of data. Data* is another word for *beliefs*. Ho'oponopono is work to clear your data.

Dr. Hew Len also said, "Have you ever noticed that when there is a problem, you are there?" That means you're a creator. You're a participator. You are a part of it. You cocreated that experience. You helped manifest this problem.

The ho'oponopono technique is Hawaiian-based. I have been to Hawaii several times, but I didn't learn about it there. I learned it from Dr. Hew Len, who learned it directly from a kahuna, a Hawaiian shaman, named Morrnah Simeona. He was so impressed that he followed her for the next twenty-five years.

You might be reluctant to accept this, but if you're 100 percent responsible for everything in your life, there's no get-out-of-jail card or permission slip. *Everything*—100 percent responsibility.

Let's look at this a little more deeply. Many people today are concerned about terrorism. How do you know that there are any terrorists out there? You read about them. You saw something about them. There was a media feed that went into your perception. That means that in some way, shape, or form, you helped create terrorism, because you created the perception that it existed. You can only experience it inside of you. So if you want to change anything, you have to do it inside of you. Your awareness of terrorism is not on the outside. It is on the inside.

Ho'oponopono corrects perception; it actually means *to make right*. We are using the technique of ho'oponopono to correct our perceptions.

If you want to talk about getting real, Dr. Hew Len was in a state hospital for the mentally insane. How much more real do you need it to be? Those patients were shackled or sedated every day. Doctors and nurses were quitting, because it was a despicable, hellish place to be. They didn't want to be there, but the state hospital still needed to have a licensed therapist on hand so it could get funding. They put out the call for someone. Dr. Hew Len, who is Hawaiian but was living in Iowa at the time, got the call and said he would do it, but he wanted permission to do his brand of therapy. They agreed, and he went to Hawaii.

Dr. Hew Len didn't see the patients. He looked at their charts. As he sits in his office looking at his charts, he reads these biographies, the lists of crimes the inmates have done, and some of them are pretty despicable. As he's looking at these very real lists, he feels what he's feeling inside himself. It's not happiness. It's rage, it's embarrassment, it's anger, it's guilt, it's grief, it's all of these different emotions.

He uses ho'oponopono on these emotions. He's doing ho'oponopono to clear his perceptions of that file on the patient. So he's looking at a file that's triggering something in him. He's using ho'oponopono to get clear of his beliefs about those people. As he does so, they start to get better. Within only a couple of months, they no longer have to be shackled or sedated. Within a few more months, some of them are pronounced as normal and released.

The doctors and nurses that were still there noticed this and said, "Dr. Hew Len, whatever you're doing for them, do it for us." They wanted to feel better too. Within four years, virtually every one of the patients was released as normal, and that ward was closed.

When I did the research for *Zero Limits*, which I coauthored with Dr. Hew Len, I found social workers who had worked in that ward at the time. I couldn't talk to the patients—I wasn't given that information because of privacy laws—but between Dr. Hew Len and the social workers, I found out just how real that place and those patients were.

If I approached you and said, "Hey, there's a hospital down the road with these patients who are criminally insane; how about you and I try to heal them?" you'd think I was nuts. You would be thinking, "Don't even go near that place. It's dangerous."

In ho'oponopono, you clear your perceptions of anything that's going on in your life. You clear your beliefs about it. As you clear your beliefs, you make it easier to get the results that you've been wanting all along.

The very simple approach to ho'oponopono is to use four statements. They are easy:

I love you.

I'm sorry.

Please forgive me.

Thank you.

Those are the four statements. You can say them in any order. You can say them with or without feeling.

Let me explain the formula here, because this is results-based, and this is how people are getting results with everything you can name. At this point, because of my two books on ho'oponopono, I've heard about people raising money for finances, overcoming fears, overcoming health problems, taking care of sick pets, dealing with their plants and their gardens and getting things to grow. The list goes on and on.

First of all, you notice that there's something wrong. You haven't gotten your result yet, or you've noticed that there's a block or a belief. In ho'oponopono, you don't have to name the belief. You just have to know that something is keeping you from your result.

The second thing is you have a communication between yourself and what I'll call the higher power. Some people call that God, the universe, Gaia, nature, but in some way, shape, or form, you are a part of something bigger than you. Even an atheist would probably say that you're part of nature. So this can be a conversation, a communion, with nature. You're making a request. You can think of it as a prayer if you like. Or you can think of it as a petition. You say those four sentences to this higher power.

You're aware of a problem or a result that you want to have. You know that there's a snag of some sort preventing you from getting there. You're going to say the four sentences as a communication to your connection to a higher power. You say them inside yourself: "I love you. I'm sorry. Please forgive me. Thank you."

What are you saying when you say that? It's a shorthand version of something longer. You're basically saying, "Please forgive me for being unconscious of my own beliefs. I'm sorry for any role I may have had, consciously or unconsciously, in the creation of this problem. Thank you for erasing the problem. Thank you for my life. Thank you for bringing me the result that I've been wanting. I love you for my life. I love you for fulfilling this request." "I love you" is the most powerful statement of all.

In a sense, you're saying a shorthand version of a longer explanation, but you're saying, "I love you. I'm sorry. Please forgive me. Thank you."

You may ask, "How many times should I say it?"

Dr. Hew Len taught me that we have so many limiting beliefs in general, not just for one particular topic but in general, that we should be saying this forever. Just say it forever.

When I first learned it, I had to make little yellow stickies and hang them up on the refrigerator and put them on the computer: *I love you. I'm sorry. Please forgive me. Thank you.*

Not long ago, I gave a talk on ho'oponopono, and a woman came up to me who had the four sentences tattooed up and down on her left arm. So do whatever you can to remind yourself of these four sentences. At some point, they become part of your new self-talk. In the back of my mind, I'm saying, "I love you. I'm sorry. Please forgive me. Thank you. I love you. I'm sorry. Please forgive me. Thank you." Why? Because I am doing my best to stay clear of limiting beliefs so that I can be present and can be the most help to people.

All of this is like a shorthand, turbocharged, Cliff Notes version of how to do ho'oponopono to get a particular result.

It's good to employ this when you feel some emotional trigger arise that might detract from getting the results you want. If you feel it, you can heal it.

This might be good for people who say, "Joe, I've tried to bring in these new beliefs, but I have this kind of automatic belief preventing me from getting the results I want."

You do not need to know the belief. You do not need to know the specifics of it. It's enough that it's been reoccurring. In fact, I think ho'oponopono works better and faster when you have a recurring problem and you're a little bit frustrated with it. So there's some emotion on it.

It's one thing to say, "I love you. I'm sorry. Please forgive me. Thank you," automatically and mindlessly. That's a fine meditation, but when you actually have your feet in the fire with some problem, that's when you can really focus and say, "I don't know what's bothering me. I don't know why I'm not getting this particular result. I don't know why I'm frustrated. I don't know what's actually going on, but—" and then you say to the higher power, to the Divine, "I'm sorry. I don't know where this belief is coming from. Please forgive me or my family or my parents or my ancestors or my epigenetics or my DNA, wherever it might have originated. Thank you for removing it and releasing it and erasing it and freeing me from it. I love you for taking care of this process and for giving me life so I can achieve this result."

Even to a skeptical person, saying, "I love you" and "Thank you" probably seems benign, but some may object to saying, "I'm sorry" and "Please forgive me" when they believe they've done nothing wrong.

In response, Dr. Hew Len said, "Look, if it makes you uncomfortable to say, 'I'm sorry,' don't say it. Just forget that one."

I have often said, "Look, all you really need to say is 'I love you.'" If you want to take "I love you" or "Thank you," or both of those, which are incredibly positive, there's enough scientific research to show that repeating these positive phrases changes your energy, your well-being, your thought pattern, your neurology. That alone is worth doing.

When my father died, people came to the funeral and said, "I'm sorry."

Why were they sorry? They didn't kill him. This is the way that you say, "I'm sorry" to the Divine or to the Great Something. You're saying, "I'm sorry that I have been unconscious, that I have been lost in beliefs and limitations that I wasn't aware of." That's all. You're not saying that you did anything wrong.

Here's another way to look at this. If you're in a crowded grocery store and you bump into somebody, don't you say, "I'm sorry"? It doesn't mean you're going to be hanged. It doesn't mean you're going to be fined or ticketed or thrown out of the store. It doesn't mean you need to feel guilty. It doesn't mean you need to feel bad at all. All you did was to go unconscious for a moment and bump into somebody. That's the mentality behind "Please forgive me" and "I'm sorry": "For a moment there, I was unconscious. I bumped into the wall. I bumped into my neighbor. Somebody passed away; I'm expressing my regret."

We take off the self-punishment. As I've said, it's about being kind to yourself and valuing yourself. So "I'm sorry" and "Please forgive me" don't have the heaviness that a lot of people associate with those statements.

To give you a final hit between the eyes: if you're having problems saying, "I'm sorry," you better do ho'oponopono on that, because you have beliefs about being sorry. You have beliefs about deservingness or guilt or punishment. You may not be able to verbalize all those beliefs, but they must be there, because it's bothering you to say something very simple: "I'm sorry. Please forgive me." So I would say all four sentences on the fact that you can't say the two sentences.

Is it more powerful to say these things verbally or silently? It's really your choice, but I have found it's more powerful to say it internally and to say only it to yourself. Never say it to another person. You never walk up to another person and say, "I'm sorry. Please forgive me. Thank you. I love you." For one thing, it'll be confusing to them, and for another, it's not how ho'oponopono works.

I have several T-shirts that have ho'oponopono phrases on them. One day I was at a gas station, and the back of my shirt said, "I love you. I'm sorry. Please forgive me. Thank you." I had forgotten about it; I was just wearing the shirt. I fellow I didn't know came up to me, and he said, "Those phrases on the back of your shirt."

"Yes?"

"Is that what you say when you're in a fight with your wife?"

I thought, and I said, "Well, I guess it would work there, too." I'm sorry. Please forgive me. Thank you. I love you."

All in all, saying it inside yourself to your connection while you're feeling emotion is the best way to do it.

There's no need to say it aloud unless you feel inspired, and there's never a need to say it to anybody else.

If you're having discord in a relationship, you might want to make these statements internally as you approach the other person. It could put you in the right frame of mind.

Another ho'oponopono teacher is a tax advisor, Mabel Katz; she's written a couple of books, and she's told stories about representing clients in front of the IRS. Here you're going into a heated situation. Many people are emotionally fueled just by seeing the letters *IRS*. They're loaded with a connotation that intimidates people.

With ho'oponopono, we learn that those are just words. We're the ones projecting all the information. Go ahead and clean on those, which is what we do with ho'oponopono. We call it *cleaning beliefs* or *clearing beliefs*. You can take care of them.

Mabel would go into the IRS office representing her client, and she would say the four phrases inside herself on what she was feeling in that moment. As a result, she won more cases than not.

In my book *Zero Limits*, I talk about a salesperson who has the most number of sales for a luxury car. When he met with people, on the surface he was using sales conversation techniques; he was doing traditional Dale Carnegie, trying to win friends and influence people. Internally, though, he was doing ho'oponopono. He was saying, "I love you. I'm sorry. Please forgive me. Thank you," on whatever he was feeling as he was trying to sell cars. This actually made it so that he wasn't trying to sell cars anymore, yet the cars got sold in the most natural way. He won awards for the most number of cars sold annually. He said that the only thing he was doing differently from the other salespeople was that he was internally cleaning, clearing, and deleting limiting beliefs using ho'oponopono.

In many ways, this is really more than a technique; it's a philosophy of life. You can do it throughout your life as your running self-talk with yourself.

Let me talk here a little about miracles. I believe in magic and miracles. My coaching program is called Miracles Coaching, and I have a book called *The Miracle*. When people ask me what a miracle is, I'll say there are two kinds.

There is the miracle of something happening that you didn't expect to happen. There's a result that you've been wanting, you've been praying for, for which you've been doing everything right, but it hasn't taken place. Then, suddenly, magically, almost mysteriously, there it is. It feels like a miracle, so you will often call that kind of sudden manifestation a miracle.

The other miracle is more important and more priceless. It is free. It is the miracle of *right now*. This is really the essence of what I teach. The miracle is now. Everything that we're longing for, searching for, scrambling for, struggling for is actually already here. It's in this moment.

Many of us get caught up in looking towards the future because we tell ourselves that it's going to be better than now. Or we look at the past and think, "That was a lot better than right now."

In both cases, we've deceived ourselves. Those are delusions.

We look at the past, but of course we don't remember it accurately. Many scientific studies prove that we're tricked by our own minds. We think things were better when they were actually worse. We think they were worse when they were actually better. We have no fair assessment of the past, so we can't really look to it. We look to the future as the possibility of creating something, which is useful as a springboard, but I learned a long time ago that the point of power is right here. The magic is right here.

The ability to create the results that you want stems from right here. The more you can be in the miracle of the now, the more you can create the results that you want in the next miracle that shows up. So for me, ho'oponopono is a direct path back to *now*. It comes through saying the four sentences and asking your higher power to delete and erase all of the beliefs that are keeping you from seeing with clarity the magic, the power, the magnificence of this moment.

CHAPTER SIX

The Third Clearing Technique: Self-Hypnosis

Some people feel that hypnosis is manipulative or unethical or akin to voodoo. Some have written over the years saying that it's ineffective. They haven't done their research.

Hypnosis is wonderful. It is a scientifically proven tool and is accepted by the American Medical Association. Dentists often use it to numb pain for people without using drugs. Hypnosis has been used for everything that you can think of.

Unfortunately, most people think in terms of stage hypnosis. Although this shows that certain parts of the mind can be influenced, it obscures how beneficial and constructive hypnosis really is. Therapists, counselors, and psychotherapists are using it for every sort of ailment—anxiety, abuse issues, obesity, insomnia. People under hypnosis have had surgery done without any numbing medication.

Unfortunately, hypnosis got off to a rocky start in the eighteenth century with the Austrian physician Franz Anton Mesmer. He was a flamboyant showman and said he used a force called *animal magnetism.* In France a scientific committee, which included Benjamin Franklin, was asked to investigate mesmerism and find out if it was actually doing anything. The committee came back and said there was nothing factual or scientific about it.

That committee didn't have access to today's technology, which reads and maps our brains and brain waves. We now know that there are stages and degrees of awakening and that you can be in a trance. In fact there's something called the *waking trance.* The waking trance means your eyes are open, so you look awake, but your mind is so focused that you don't really know where you are.

Virtually everybody can relate to highway hypnosis: you're driving for a very long time, and suddenly you realize, "I think that was my exit." You were in a waking hypnotic trance. At that point, your mind was occupied by something else, and you missed your exit.

For our purposes, we're looking for a way to construct a reality that will bring us our result. We will mentally manufacture our result with visualization.

Remember the reticular activating system. We have repeatedly fouled it with negative imagery, so we need to reprogram it to bring us our desired result.

Hypnosis is a wonderful way to reprogram the reticular activating system. It's also great for removing limiting beliefs. When we find them, we can go in and create a different narrative. We can even use self-hypnosis to give the command to ourselves to release a belief.

You don't have to go to a therapist. You certainly don't have to go on stage. This is something you learn to do for yourself; it's very simple, easy, and safe. Because you're doing hypnosis for yourself, you're not manipulating yourself, unless you want to say that manipulating yourself is moving you in the direction of your own dreams. You're not going to do anything harmful to yourself, because you're going for a result that you want, something that's beneficial to you and your family, friends, and probably the community, if not the planet.

I can say a lot about hypnosis. My company is called Hypnotic Marketing, which is also the title of one of my books; another is called *Hypnotic Writing*. I've also written about hypnotic storytelling. I have been hypnotized; I have practiced hypnosis; I have hypnotized others.

Hypnosis is slightly different from visualization, which is a tool to be used within hypnosis. Think of hypnosis as a relaxation technique, as a way to sharpen your attention so that you can focus on the results you want. You can focus on relaxing. You can focus on using tools like visualization, but you are controlling your own mind. With hypnosis, you are relaxing, you are focusing, and you are targeting a result you want.

I would actually say that we're all in a trance of one sort or another, even right now. The first time I was on *Larry King*, he was promoting the movie *The Secret*, and he was talking about trances. I said, "We're all in a trance. We have the trance of vocation. We think we are a particular thing. I am an author. I am a speaker. I am a housewife. I am a business owner. I am a baker. I am a mother of three." Those "I am" statements reflect trances.

It's easy to go into a trance. TV knows how to program us. Television and the people behind it know how to create the very things that the reticular activating system responds to. They're creating *images* that captivate us. They create *emotion*, which stamps that image on our reticular activating system. They *repeat* the images over and over again throughout the shows. Music too can program you, usually unconsciously.

The mass media are programming their shows in ways that are very hypnotic. I don't think this is bad in itself. I don't know that any of the people behind the programs are intentionally trying to brainwash people or put them into trances. I think they're doing this inadvertently, but as people who are awakening, who want to get clear and get better results, we need to be aware of this programming and then consciously choose what we want to pay attention to.

I don't have a TV set at this point, but if I wanted to watch TV, I would choose what I watch, and as I enjoyed it, I'd be paying attention to how it might be programming me. People often make a unconscious mistake when they watch TV: they unconsciously conclude that this is how life is. Then they create dramas in their life so they have the same kind of excitement that they saw on TV.

This is an example of unconscious programming. Viewers are creating beliefs, much as I did when I was homeless: I admired Jack London, Ernest Hemingway, and other self-destructive authors, so I unconsciously became self-destructive.

In all these cases, we want to become aware of the programming. It is a form of hypnosis; it puts us in a trance. Does this trance serve you or not? If it doesn't, it's time to awaken from it and move into a different trance. If it does, then enjoy the ride. Keep on going to get the results that you want.

Television is entertainment, but it's also programming. The media call them programs unconsciously, not knowing that they're programming us.

One of the greatest things you can do for your own well-being is turn off the mainstream news. Turn off the TV. You can be selective about what you want to watch, but for the most part it's going to deeply influence you. If you're not aware of the buttons that are being rewired within you, you will become a walking programmed robot.

The news media know how to go out and find the scariest stuff. If there isn't something scary in your neighborhood, they'll go and find it in the next state over. If they don't find anything there, they'll find it somewhere else in the nation. They're looking for something to scare you. Why? Your reticular activating system is programmed for survival. If there is an alert for you to be afraid, an alert that you might be in danger, you need to be aware of it so you can do something to save your life.

The media manipulate that tendency. They make you afraid. Now they have your attention. Now they can feed you truths, lies, facts, beliefs, commercials, advertising. You are now wide open because these things have grabbed your attention. Furthermore, the media will keep doing it, which is repetition. So as long as you keep tuning in, you keep getting programmed. This will be effective until you awaken to the idea that it is programming.

One time I picked up Dr. Hew Len while we were writing the first book, *Zero Limits*, and I asked him, "What were you doing this afternoon?"

"I was watching TV."

"What were you watching?"

"The news."

"Oh my God," I said, "why would you watch that? I tell everybody to turn the news off."

"Because I wanted to clean on what was being triggered in me."

He was using TV news as a tool to find out where his beliefs, his buttons, and his triggers were; as he found them, he used ho'oponopono to erase them. He was in a different place with the television set than me. I find it easier to leave it off or not to have one at all.

To go back to self-hypnosis: level one is the conscious mind, and level two is the subconscious mind. The conscious mind is the top level, the tip of the iceberg. Most people think that this is what's creating their results in life. But it's not the conscious mind; it's the subconscious/unconscious. It's the larger part of the iceberg, which is below the surface. The conscious mind is just the tip.

The work needs to be done in the subconscious/unconscious mind. That's where the drivers are. If you have beliefs about money, for example, that little tip of the iceberg is thinking, "I want money." You write it on the tip of the iceberg, but underneath it are beliefs, which can be anything: "I don't believe it's possible." "I don't think I deserve it." "There's a shortage." "Money corrupts."

The subconscious/unconscious is where all of those beliefs are. Ho'oponopono works with the data in the iceberg below conscious awareness. Self-hypnosis does the same thing.

Self-hypnosis uses the conscious mind to get to the subconscious. You go to a hypnotist and say, "I want you to hypnotize me. I'm trying to achieve a particular result, but I feel these beliefs are in the way. Take me under, and move around the wiring of these beliefs."

That's in effect what you do with self-hypnosis, only it's something you can do yourself. We want to use self-hypnosis to make a result happen. We declare what the result is with our conscious mind. We might be able to find out our beliefs just by thinking about what our intent is. Then we go into the subconscious mind with a self-hypnosis technique. We reformat that part of our brain, release the limiting beliefs, replace them with new ones if need be, and then come out of it to let the new programming seep into the conscious mind and create a new reality.

Let's do this as simply as possible. First of all, we want to remove any emotional charge from the word *hypnosis*. I'm talking about relaxation. When you relax, you have access to your subconscious mind; you have access to inspiration. Your stress has kept you from tapping into it. You want to cross this invisible conscious/subconscious mind barrier by asking your conscious mind to tell your subconscious mind to relax. You can relax by giving it something to focus on.

Traditional hypnotists would put a candle up and would ask you to look at the flame. I have a hypnotist's cane from nineteenth-century France. It has a removable crystal on the top, and inside is a candle. The hypnotist would put the candle down, light it, and invite you to gaze at it as a way to focus your attention. The cane also has a little gold watch—the old method of hypnotizing by having the subject look at the watch. What are these tools for? Are they just tricks? No, they are ways to focus the mind.

When you're driving and you go into highway hypnosis, your mind has been occupied by the road. It became so boring and repetitive that your mind has wandered off, but your body still knows to keep in the lane and keep driving. It also knows where your exit is; it tells you either just in the nick of time or just as you've passed it.

Here, you're consciously saying, "I want to relax. Subconscious mind, I want you to relax." Let's walk you through how to do it. My favorite way is progressive relaxation. If I have trouble sleeping, I use progressive relaxation to fall asleep.

With this technique, you're lying in bed, although you can sit up if you want. You consciously tell your toes to relax. You just give them the command. (In hypnosis, you're always giving commands.) You might wiggle them a little bit so you can feel them, but you only take a second there. Then you progressively go to the next part, which could be the soles of your feet, the arches, the heels, the ankles. You're slowly and progressively moving up your body, inviting it to relax.

You're consciously inviting and seducing the subconscious, the physical body, to relax. You're going up your legs, your thighs, your whole body. Usually I find that when I get somewhere close to my midsection, I'm asleep. The next morning I wake up and say, "Where was I when I was doing the progressive relaxation? Somewhere around the stomach I disappeared."

It's brilliant to record your own voice in order to do this. You would record your own voice, saying, "OK, Joe, let's lie down. Let's relax. Let's take a few deep breaths. Then let's look at our toes. Let's relax our toes. Let's relax the soles of our feet."

Speak slowly, with pauses. Go through your whole body this way, speaking more and more slowly. When you get to the part where your whole body is relaxed, that's when you can give commands to the subconscious. "I now sleep easily and effortlessly every night, and every night I get better and better about falling asleep faster and faster." Or, "I now believe that the more money I spend, the more money I receive," or any other statement or affirmation you want to adopt. It doesn't matter if you fall asleep or not, because that deeper part of you is listening anyway.

You can put five or ten commands in there. You can repeat them a few times. Repetition is something the reticular activating system likes. Then leave a little bit of time for rest or sleep.

Finally you begin to awaken. You can say, "When you awaken, it will be at the count of five. When I get to five, you'll be more relaxed than ever." You're just giving another command. "You will be alert, you'll know where you are. You'll have your bearings and your surroundings. Your eyes will be wide open, and a big smile will be on your face." All of these are commands about how you want to feel.

Then, at the end, clap your hands or snap your fingers and say, "OK, awaken."

That's how easy self-hypnosis can be.

The more you get into hypnosis, the more you realize that you can trust yourself: you can trust your subconscious/unconscious mind. I am a student of Milton Erickson, who was one of the great modern hypnotists. He was a very eccentric fellow but was known to get amazing results. He taught himself to trust his own unconscious mind, and he taught other people to trust theirs. When you realize you have your own answers, you gain confidence. You might have to use ho'oponopono or some of the other clearing techniques that I'm describing, but you will have more confidence in them the more you realize that you do have inner wisdom coming from your unconscious. Great results will come from that.

Inspirational author Wayne Dyer once did an exercise that shows the magic of the mind. He said, "Visualize a beautiful rose bush. Can you see it in your mind?"

People would say, "Yes, there's the rose bush."

"Now visualize a young puppy sleeping; you can hear it breathing."

"Oh, yes, I got the young puppy, it's breathing, and it's so beautiful and sweet."

Then Wayne Dyer said, "I'll give you $10,000 if you can tell me how you did that. How did you switch from rose to puppy in your brain? How did you get this crystal-clear, beautiful flower in one moment, and a split second later, you're looking at a puppy? How did that happen in your mind?"

This story shows the magic of what's available in our brain, and also how mysterious it is, because Dyer never had to give his $10,000 away. Nobody could break this process down in any mechanical, scientific way.

When you think about this, you realize you can have confidence in your subconscious, because it has answers. It has power. It has wisdom. It has connections that you don't have consciously. This is where intuition and inspiration come from.

With self-hypnosis, you tune out the rest of the world by tuning in to the result you want. Then there is *future pacing*: you are sitting in this reality, but you are imagining down the road into the future, where you can say, "I have my result now." When you imagine that you have your result—which could be next week or next month or next year—you can start to imagine how real it is. It's not just a figment of your imagination. You've created it in your mind, and it's very vivid. Your reticular activating system is now aware of its concreteness. You're future-pacing a reality by being in this moment, being relaxed, and communicating with your powerful subconscious mind. You do it by being totally tuned into this thing and tuned out from the rest of the world.

Out of that, you plant this signal into your brain: "This is the result I want." All this can happen in a self-hypnosis session. It's powerful. Miracles that can happen from this.

Here's another way of using self-hypnosis to eliminate a limiting belief.

When I was going to be on stage for the first time as a singer/songwriter with my band, I was terrified. When I told people this, they thought I was kidding. They said, "You've been on stage many times in front of many audiences all around the world, and in movies and on TV."

"Yes," I said, "but not as a singer."

I was going to perform at the Townsend, which is a nightclub in Austin, Texas. I thought, "Is there any way for me to get out of this? I can't. I'm the guy who teaches face your fears and have courage and believe in miracles and dissolve your beliefs and get results. How can I get out of this? I can't. I have to do this."

So what did I do? First I did virtually every clearing technique that I'm describing in this book, but I also used self-hypnosis. I created an alter ego, a fearless public singer. I even created a name and a story for him. Antonio Bembe.

Antonio Bembe came from Cuba. He escaped Cuba in the sixties, after Castro took power. He was a young boy at the time. He showed signs of being a singer, but he didn't get a chance to do it in Cuba. He came to the United States, and he couldn't speak English, but he learned. Antonio made money by singing on street corners; enough people liked him that he was invited to a couple of clubs. Then he was invited to sing at bigger arenas.

He starts wearing a white suit with a white tie, and a panama hat. He becomes quite the ladies' man. He's fearless on stage. Antonio holds the crowd. Antonio sings, his band comes up behind him, and people get chills. Women faint. Men get envious. It is amazing what takes place when Antonio owns the stage.

That was a self-hypnosis trance I created for myself. When I went on stage with my band, I knocked them dead. I got a standing ovation.

Nobody knew about Antonio; I didn't tell other people about him, but I do now, after the fact. I used self-hypnosis. I put myself into a progressively relaxed state. I started to imagine Antonio, whom I invented out of my own brain. What would he be like? What would he sound like? Then I future-paced myself stepping into him as a character. What would it be like if I were Antonio?

Pretending you have an alter ego brings out latent talents in you that you didn't even know were there. It's like having a role model, except that you already have the qualities that you admire. The alter ego helps pull them out.

I used self-hypnosis, with that imagery, to get the result I wanted. I would advise you to do something similar. Again, there are hundreds, if not thousands, of ways to do hypnosis to get the results you want. This happens to be a really cool one, and anybody can do it.

So if I were afraid of public speaking, I'd ask myself, "Who are some of the greatest speakers?" I might think of Mark Twain, who was known as a fantastic speaker. I might think of John F. Kennedy. I might think of Martin Luther King. I might think of different people in my own life. Think of them and then ask, "What are they doing? What are their traits?"

When Martin Luther King gave his famous "I Have a Dream" speech, he had seven pages of notes. He didn't use them. He was sitting there beforehand, reviewing his notes, and someone in the crowd who had heard him speak said, "Hey, King, tell them about the dream." He stood up and improvised that famous speech. He trusted himself and his past experience. He trusted his subconscious.

Some of the skill comes from experience, and some of it comes from role playing: "If I were Antonio Bembe, how would I be on stage?" In any event, self-hypnosis unleashes a wonderful part of you that has been shackled.

CHAPTER SEVEN

The Fourth
Clearing Technique:
Healing Music

As I've mentioned, I decided around the age of
sixty to be a musician. It was on my bucket list. I
looked at my life and said, "You've accomplished
quite a bit. What do you want to do now?" I thought, "I've
always wanted to play music."

I did play the harmonica, which is a nice little fireside
instrument, and it's fun to play. I could play blues impro-
visationally, but I wanted to play guitar; I wanted to write
songs; I wanted to go into the studio. I had a fantasy of

recording my own album. It's a wild fantasy. There was nobody saying, "Go do this." This was just something coming from me.

I decided that I was going to be a musician. I would learn to sing and play the guitar and write songs. I would learn how to go in the studio with a band and put some tracks down.

Guess what happened. Deep terror. Fear. Why? Because whenever you attempt to do something new, you're going to be uncomfortable. If I decide that I'm going to start mountain climbing, the next thing that's going to happen is that all of my fears about climbing mountains, being athletic, having endurance, having the skills, are going to come to the surface. If I don't clear those, I won't climb a mountain.

It was the same thing with music. I knew that the terror that was coming up was exactly what happens for everybody who has decided, "Here's the result I want." This is why I say one of the first things to do is state your intention. What's your result that you want? State it. Write it down, because the next thing that comes up is all of the limiting beliefs. That's when you bring in the tools to clear them.

I had to do the same thing. I was terrified: "How can I do this? I don't sing in the shower. I don't sing behind the wheel of the car. I'm not going to be able to sing in the studio. I don't know how to play the guitar. I only know a couple of chords, and I don't what to do with them."

I started using all of the techniques in this book— including ones that we haven't gotten to yet—to get rid of my limiting beliefs. Not only did I collapse all of those beliefs, but I did it in record time, to the extent that I have recorded fifteen albums in about five years.

I'm not saying this to brag; I'm saying it as a teaching tale. When you collapse those beliefs, when you get clear of them, you can accelerate the path to the results you want. That's what I've done with music.

I have become a healing musician. I've called myself the world's first self-help singer/songwriter. Part of that is just thinking like a marketer. I've written books like *Hypnotic Marketing*, and I've been known as a copywriter and Internet marketer. I wrote a book on P. T. Barnum— *There's a Customer Born Every Minute*—so there's a marketing side to my life.

When I started to think about creating my own music, I thought, "What makes my music different? There's are 1,000 to 3,000 new albums every week." How do you stand out in the crowd?

When I looked out there to see what was already being produced, I thought, "Hey, there's nobody doing self-help music." So I called myself a self-help musician, and I said I was creating healing music.

On one level, it's just a marketing angle. It's a way to hang my hat on something different; it's a way to stand out in the marketplace. On another level, though, it's a clearing technique that actually works.

Let's go back to the concept of programming television. We, unconsciously and without question, download statements that are being made to us by the media. We take these on, and we fall into fear. We start to think that there's scarcity in the world. We start to think that the world is out to get us.

Music does the same thing. One example is from the Rolling Stones. I love the Rolling Stones; I love their music; I love the fact that they've been around for decades. But a lot of people are saying to themselves, "I just can't get what I want. I'm trying everything. I'm reading the books, watching the movies, doing everything I'm being asked to do, but I can't get what I want."

Then it occurred to me: "Gosh, the Rolling Stones sang that to us in the 1960s: You can't always get what you want." They sang it repeatedly, and everybody has heard that song and probably can sing it. We don't realize that they are singing affirmations right into our brain, and we accept them without question, because it's a catchy lyric. A lot of us nod our heads and say, "Yeah, I can't always get what I want."

Here is the big takeaway: become aware of how music is programming you. If you are listening to lyrics that are making you feel down or depressed or discouraged, that music is not uplifting you. It's not aiming you in the direction of getting the results you want.

When you are learning the harmonica, one of the first places you go is to blues music, because the harmonica is used a lot in the blues, but I noticed early on that a lot of blues music is sad. It reinforces the belief that you are broke, you are alone. All there is is your beer and your dog. It's some of the saddest stuff, but again, it's catchy. It's easy to listen to. It goes right into your being.

Here's your wakeup call: this music is programming you for lack and limitation. Now, much like when you watch television, if you can be aware that there is programming here, it doesn't necessarily have to program you, because you're aware. But when we are unconscious, when we absorb this information without questioning it, it becomes part of our programming. It becomes part of the software of the mind.

We want to be aware of that. We want to more consciously choose the lyrics we want to hear. This is why I have six singer/songwriter albums at this point, and the songs on those albums are written by me. I'm trying to create the alternative: I'm trying to create positive music. I'm trying to create happy music. I'm trying to create lyrics that have the same memorable quality and the same captivating music as those of the Rolling Stones, but programs you in a much more positive way so you can get the results you want.

On my latest album, *The Great Something,* I have a song called "The Glad Game." The idea is that in every moment and in every person, there is always something good. This goes back to 1913, with Eleanor H. Porter's famous book, *Pollyanna*, which has been turned into several different movies and TV shows over the years. Little Pollyanna was taught to play the "Glad Game": no matter what was going on, you would look at the situation, and you would find something to be glad about.

Admittedly, sometimes it would take a minute or two. You'd look at a situation and think, "There's nothing good in that one," but you'd take a breath, pause, dig a little deeper, and ask, "OK, how might this play out?"

Coach Kurt Wright said, "Have you ever noticed that a year after a negative event, you often saw the humor in it, and you often saw that you could laugh about it and you could tell a story with a punch line that made everybody giggle?" Then he went on to say, "If the humor exists a year after the negative event, didn't it exist in the moment of the negative event? You just weren't ready to see it yet."

I read *Pollyanna*, and I thought, "This is amazing. People don't grasp how powerful a clearing technique this is, because when people get caught up in the negative, they don't get the results they want. They've been gumming up their own mental processes. They no longer have the clarity to see their options or opportunities." When you play the Glad Game, you look at what's possible. You look at freedom of choice, because you're looking for something good.

I wrote a song about the Glad Game because I'm trying to help people to look in that direction. I'm not the only person doing this. There are the Posi Awards, which are for positive music. In fact, I think my songs "The Glad Game" and "The Great Something" were nominated. The point is there's a lot of happy, healing music that can clear us to go in the direction of our dreams.

Jason Mraz is one of my favorite singer/songwriters, because he tends to write nothing but happy music. This is the point of healing music. You want to feel good. You want your energy to go up. From a scientific standpoint, you want the endorphins in your brain to be firing so that you feel happier. You want the dopamine to be going through your bloodstream so that you feel you can accomplish any result that you want.

A recent song by Jason Mraz has the line, "I want you to have it all." Every time I hear that song, even now, I am smiling, just thinking, "I want you to have it all. I want me to have it all." When I listen to that song, I have a buoyancy in my spirit. I actually put it on my Facebook page as my favorite song so that when people go there, they can ride the wave of that endorphin rush.

Music that can do this for us is a treasure. There is an overwhelming amount of positive music available, with lyrics or without lyrics, that people can choose.

My point with this is to be aware of how music influences your body and mind. Then choose wisely so you get the results you want.

It's sad statement that for many people "Pollyanna" has become an insult. When you hear someone say, "You're a Pollyanna," it means, "You're simplistic. You see only joy where there's clearly suffering. You're being blind to reality."

Eleanor Porter said, "*Pollyanna* did not dismiss the reality of pain and suffering in the world. *Pollyanna* did not say there were no bad things or things you would want to change. *Pollyanna* said that there is good in the world, and if you took a moment to find it, you could enlarge on it."

If I look out into the world, I definitely see things we need to resolve. I was homeless at one point, and I walk around in big cities and see homeless people all over the place. Not all of them want to be off the streets, but enough of them do that we can do something about it.

From a realistic Pollyanna standpoint, I say, "Yes, there is a real problem there. What is the good that is happening? There are good people trying to make a difference, and what good can I do?"

A few years ago, I started a movement called Operation Yes. It's a movement to end homelessness in the United States. I have a book called *Operation Yes* for people who are struggling. It's on Amazon, and it's free at operationyes.com.

You can play that game of telling yourself, "There's so much bad in the world. Why try to do anything? I'm just going to roll over and give up on my results." But that's a form of self-sabotage. That's a form of escape. That's creating an excuse to let you off the hook so you don't go for the result that you really want.

My commitment is to give people tools so they can finally have the results they want in life. The whole Pollyanna phrase is a simple tool to help you look at what's already working for you. Where are you already getting results? Where's the positive that's already taking place in your life? When you focus on the positive, you get more positive. When you focus on your strengths, you get more of them, and you enlarge them. This is a different way of being in the world.

Whether you're listening to background instrumental music or you're listening to music with lyrics, you want to be aware of how it influences you. Everything is influencing you—TV, music, other people's conversations, and of course, your own thinking. My song "The Glad Game" is a reminder to look for the good in each moment.

Some people ask, "Isn't it possible to listen to music for entertainment purposes only, with a conscious understanding that you like the melody, but not the message?"

When I go in the gym to work out, I listen, for example, to a song by Shaman's Harvest that says, "I am dangerous." On one level, you might think that you don't want that song out there in the world, but on another level, you think, "I'm going to the gym. I'm going to bend metal. I'm going to do some superhuman struggling, muscular activities. I need to have that edge. For the next twenty minutes, I need to have the mind-set, at least secretly, that I am dangerous."

Then there's Melissa Etheridge. I studied music with her. In fact the title of my album *The Great Something* came from my interaction with her. I was originally going to call it *The Miracle*, but she said, "That's kind of overused."

"Well, I sometimes refer to the Divine or the higher power as the Great Something."

"There's real intrigue in that," she said. So I wrote the song "The Great Something" and gave the same name to the album. It even has a song for her called "Melissa Said."

At one point Melissa wrote a song called "Monster." I listened to it, and there's a great melody and a rock beat to it, but it is all about being a monster. On one level, I don't want to be a monster, but when I go in the gym, I do kind of want to be a monster. So what do you want to listen to that might empower the alter ego to be superhuman, at least long enough to get your workout done? This is where you have to have your own discernment, your own inner judge to find out whether this is serving you or slowing you down.

Tony Robbins plays loud, blaring rock music before he goes on stage. He wants everybody on their feet. He wants the adrenaline pumping. He wants the energy soaring. He wants to lift the roof off the place. At that point we're listening to the melody; we're not really listening to the message.

So you want to pay attention to how music is influencing you personally. I'll listen to "Monster" or "I Am Dangerous" when I'm working out at the gym because I want to engage more of my energy. I might listen to something softer, like "The Glad Game," or the song I wrote called "There'll Be Days."

Queen's "Bohemian Rhapsody" is a great song (and movie) but they end it with, "Nothing really matters," which certainly looks negative. Let's think deeply about this. You know what? Nothing really does matter. When I go to Rome and I look at the ruins there, I see it's all gone. In thousands of years, our achievements are all going to be dust, and there won't be any record of us. Maybe people from other planets will try to figure out what our lives were like, but we'll be gone. On one level, nothing really matters.

When I did a self-improvement course decades ago, they wanted you to get to that place where nothing really matters, because when you're at that place, you're free to choose what you really want. You're free to say, "What kind of result do I want in my life?" You are free to pick anything, and that is very empowering.

On the other hand, you can also say that on some level everything, every thought that you put in your mind, matters in terms of your results. So in some ways both sides of that coin can be true.

I wrote and recorded a song called, "There'll Be Days." The studio and everybody involved in my band told me that it's a stellar song because it is speaking true wisdom. That's what I really want in healing music—to remind myself of some of the truths of life. That particular song does that.

Another song of mine, "The Healing Song," is designed to be a combination of self-hypnosis and clearing statements. It uses a metaphor of a healing well to help people clear a problem or belief that is keeping them from getting the result they want. I wrote it out with the hypnotist part of me. I wrote it to speak to a person's subconscious/unconscious mind to say, "I know that there's a problem going on." Then I go through a metaphor in which they step into a healing well, which will erase their negative programming. We actually hired a Grammy award-winning cello player, David Darling, to write and play the music for it. This is my healing poem, and it is incredibly powerful because it's speaking to your subconscious mind. In fact, recently a friend of mine who was suffering with a lot of different illnesses remembered "The Healing Song." She started listening to it and had profound experiences of beliefs being released. In this case, she was working on healing her physical body. A physical breakthrough was taking place from "The Healing Song."

When I was first learning about writing songs, I heard that there were basically three categories of songs: "I just fell in love," "I just fell out of love," and "Let's party." I would say that the music about falling in love and partying, enjoying life, is in the direction of what you want to listen to.

Start exploring. When I'm driving, I listen to satellite radio, and I just punch in stations in the categories that I like. Sometimes I want jazz music because I play a little bit of saxophone, so I want to listen to jazz to hear what the saxophone is doing. Sometimes I'll listen to popular music, but I'm looking for new artists that are saying positive things that resonate with me personally.

One more thought comes to mind: Be open to creating your own music. Be open to improvisational musical therapy. When I was in Italy, a friend of mine said he wanted to play an instrument. He tried a couple of times with the piano, but it didn't really work for him. I was in a music store; I saw a harmonica and thought, "You know, a harmonica is like a minipiano. Those ten little holes are like ten little keys."

I bought it for him as a gift. He blew a few notes on it and said, "Oh, I love this." With the harmonica in particular, you can make music pretty easily. If somebody tells you how to blow and draw through it, the next thing you know, you can make music with it.

There is the ukulele, which is so much fun to play, and you can do it with scaled-down chords. You don't have to learn a lot of chords; you can learn one or two. Actually you don't have to learn any of them. You can just entertain yourself with it.

I think it was comedian Steve Martin who said, "Any time you pick up a banjo, you laugh and you smile. There's something about the banjo that just makes you smile." I've never played the banjo, but he has a point there.

Think about the kind of instrument that might make you happy. You don't have to master it. Just play it in an improvisational way that might be therapeutic to you. It might give you the ability to distract or program your mind in order to dissolve some unwanted beliefs.

Scientific research says that when you occupy your conscious mind, your subconscious mind has a chance to heal and resolve issues, solve problems, and create breakthroughs. You're distracting the conscious mind so that the bottom of the iceberg can do some work. Playing an instrument is one way to distract the conscious mind.

It doesn't have to be music with lyrics. Instrumental music can be far more beneficial for creativity, for relaxation, for going to sleep at night, for resolving problems. In fact, if I'm working on a blog post or writing my next book, I do not listen to music with lyrics. It will distract me. I will listen to instrumental music.

Six of my fifteen albums are singer/songwriter albums, so those have lyrics, but all the other ones are instrumentals. In the other ones, which I've done with Guitar Monk Mathew Dixon, I'll play guitar; sometimes I'll play the synthophone, which is an alto saxophone that has been enhanced with internal electronics. You can play almost any kind of sound through it.

We've created instrumental tracks, even at different frequencies. We have one called "432 to Zero." All the music is tuned to the 432 frequency, which some science is suggesting is the more natural, relaxed state for us. It attunes us to the universe or to the vibe of the planet, if you will. When you listen to that kind of music, you relax faster, you create better, you resolve problems more easily. It is less distracting than music with lyrics.

A lot of research says that classical music is very powerful. Some studies have shown that when newborn babies listen to classical music played in the background, their brains develop faster.

Again, it's paying attention to what's the result you want. If I'm writing, I'm going to listen to instrumental music. If I want to go into the gym or go for a walk or a drive, I'm going to select music that is going to be applicable to what I'm trying to do.

In the morning, look at how you want to feel. That sets the tone for the day. One morning recently I listened to a song that I had heard on a flight back from Thailand; it was called "Strange People." It had an upbeat, fast-track, rock feel, and I started giggling a little bit. It was making me feel different. I had just woken up. I hadn't even had my coffee yet. I put on this song, and my energy went up. I felt better; I felt more aligned. I was ready for my day, and I giggled, thinking, "I need to do this every morning."

On the other end of the day, I don't want to be listening to rock music when I'm about to go to sleep. I want to listen to relaxing music, such as classical or instrumental. I will even listen to pink noise—background noise that sounds like a fan running or water dribbling down off the roof. It's all to get one result: relaxation.

To sum it up, I'd say, look at the result you want and the music that helps you achieve it. Then start now. Start in the morning. What do you want to listen to? Find out what works for you and then start doing it.

CHAPTER EIGHT

The Fifth Clearing Technique: Mentoring and Coaching

You can't do it all alone. You need to stretch. You need to learn more about what you're doing and why you're doing it. You need to get out of your nest of beliefs.

We're living out of a belief-driven universe, but we don't know what our beliefs are, because we think they are reality. We look around, and we see what we see, thinking, "That's the end of it. That's the limit of what's possible."

When you get a coach or a mentor, when you're involved with other people, you can begin to see other possibilities. You can begin to question beliefs that you didn't even know you had. You can begin to dissolve limits that you didn't know were there. You need a coach, a mentor to see your own limitations and get out of them.

Mentoring, coaching, or mastermind is a little-known but powerful and priceless secret of getting results. (*Mastermind* is a term coined by Napoleon Hill in *Think and Grow Rich*. He defines it as a "coordination of knowledge and effort, in a spirit of harmony, between two or more people.") When I was growing up in the 1950s, the only coaches were the football coach and the coaches on TV. I don't think personal-development coaches were around at that time, but if they were, I certainly never heard of them.

Now, decades later, lots of people say they're coaches or mentors, or start mastermind groups. All of this is valuable. One secret to success is to have somebody who believes in you almost more than you believe in yourself.

Throughout my life, I have run into people—in most cases through synchronicity—who saw something in me that I didn't yet see in myself. Because they saw it and helped develop it, they became coaches and mentors before I even knew what those words meant.

When I was sixteen, I was struggling with whether I wanted to be author, a magician, or a variety of things. At that time there was a famous magician named John Mulholland, who had known Harry Houdini. Although at that point he was up in age, he was still a full-time magician. He had written a number of books and edited a number of magical magazines. He was a very well-known, well-respected man.

I wrote to him out of the blue; this was in 1970, I believe. I typed a letter to him on my Smith Corona electric typewriter and sent it off to an address I had in New York. I told him, "I'm sixteen. This is what I'm struggling with. What kind of advice do you have?"

I still have the two-page letter he wrote back (it has been published in *Magic Magazine*, because it's a historical document); he answered all of my questions. He pointed out by being a magician, I would learn a great deal about science, performance, speaking, and entrepreneurship. He also said that by being a magician, I would have many other struggles—getting work, being an independent entrepreneur, getting bookings and gigs, dealing with the competition.

It was pure coaching. It was pure mentoring. It helped me look at my question from a lot of different angles. It's priceless for me: as a sixteen-year-old nobody, I wrote to a legendary magician, and he wrote me back two pages of advice.

Let me go forward to a point where I'm still struggling. I'm out of homelessness, but I'm still in poverty. Because of a fluke, I meet a man (it may have been at a party). He sees something in me and says, "I'm a coach. I would like to give you a coaching session."

"*Give* me?"

"I want you to sample it. I want you to get a sense of what I do, and if you like it, if we connect with each other, we can do it long-term."

At the first session, I was very nervous and uncertain. I didn't know what coaching was or who he was. We talked about my goals: what results did I want to get in my life? At that point, I was still a struggling author. I wanted to be published.

I had a book published in 1984, but it came and went with the wind. I celebrated the moment, but I was disappointed because the moment came and went. Yet I still wanted to be an author.

I was struggling with money. I was struggling to pay $200 a month to live in a room and driving a clunker of a car. When it broke down, my life broke down; there was no hope, no light. I couldn't play the Glad Game, because my mind didn't go there. I didn't know how to look for the good.

I went to see the coach, and he pointed out something that had never occurred to me. (This is the power of coaching right here.) I was trying to make all of my money from writing. He said, "Income is a big circle. It can come through any number of doors."

I'd wanted it to come through one door only—writing. When he first brought it up, I thought, "Yes, that's the only door I've got—the writing door. That's my door of income, because I'm a writer." He was coaching me to expand my mind, to see that there were other opportunities. Of course I couldn't name the other opportunities right there in that moment, because that was my first session with him, and it was my first taste of new possibilities.

As I went to this coach, I realized that my past programming, while it was not negative in and of itself, caused me to be limited in seeing possibilities. It caused me to see only one door to making money. Through him, I started to see there were other doors. I couldn't name them yet, but they existed, and there were windows too, and escape hatches.

In further sessions with this coach, I started to see my beliefs about deserving. I started to see that a part of me didn't really want to be successful because I didn't think I deserved it. I started to realize that my homelessness had left my self-esteem at zero. I'd gotten married in 1979 because I was lonely, and the woman I met was lonely. We were two lonely people who solved the loneliness problem, but we didn't solve the poverty problem. We struggled horribly, and I was embarrassed by that. I wasn't able to provide. According to my upbringing, I was supposed to be the source of income, to be the hero, but we were both flat on our face.

Through coaching, I became aware of my own limiting beliefs about myself, my sense of undeservingness, my lack of appreciation for my life and my well-being. On another level, I was punishing myself, saying, "If I'm not good enough for success, I'll keep wallowing in misery as a punishment."

I became aware of all of this because of coaching. When I did, I could do something about it. I could look in the mirror and start to see the things that I appreciated. Again, it's about learning how to love and appreciate yourself, taking an inventory of the things you're doing right, your past experiences, your strengths. All of this is to build up a muscle of confidence within yourself. I had to do all of that, but I was doing it under a coach. There was somebody holding my hand.

When somebody believes in you even before you believe in yourself, your self-esteem starts to rise. Something clicks within that says, "I must have something going on, because he or she believes in me."

When you start to realize what your limiting beliefs are, you're at the point where you can make choices. Do I want to continue being in misery? No. Do I want to continue to look just at one door of possibilities for wealth? No, I'm curious what the other doors are.

Through coaching you expand your mind, you become more aware; you also get new tools. A cascade of wonderful little miracles takes place, leading to better and better.

I swear that coaching is the reason for my success. Sure, I've had to do the work. I've had to write the books and record the music and get on the planes to travel. Yes, I've had to do all of that, but it was coaching that enabled me to break through my limitations to get the results I want. I still use coaches today, because whenever you try for something new, you're going to hit limits.

What qualities should look you for in a coach? The first thing is to find a coach that has already gotten the results that you want. Either they got these results themselves, or they helped other people get them. They already have proven personal experience in getting these results.

When I'm learning how to sing, I want to go to a voice coach who has already helped other newbies learn how to sing.

The second thing is "By their fruits you will know them." Look at their students. Who has used this coach before? Look at the testimonials. Look at the endorsements that they've gotten. If you like, go and talk to a few of the coach's other clients and find out what that experience was like.

The third thing is to look at their credentials. There are too many weekend coaches. A lot of ads out there say, "Learn how to be a life coach in two days." I don't want a person with that training as my life coach, because I don't believe they've had the skills or the experience to be of real value to me.

In short, look at who got the results that you want to get. What endorsements and credentials do they have? Where did they get their training? Study their website, and pay attention to how you feel about it. The next step is to talk to them or visit with them with a free consultation.

Let me give you an example. Recently I went through the death of my father, and I was experiencing pain, grief, and guilt. Of course I used the techniques I'm describing in this book, but at a certain point I hit a wall. When you hit the wall, you raise your hand and say, "I need help. I need a coach. I need a mentor."

I started thinking about whom I would like to have help me. At that time I was reading a couple of books by Dr. Fredric Mau. I was very impressed. I liked where he was coming from. He talked about hypnosis and self-hypnosis. He had ten years of experience working with big problems and little problems. He's worked with people who have been abused, who have gone through divorce, grief, and many other issues. The more I looked at his materials, the more I thought, "I think I might want to work with him."

I looked up his website. I liked what I saw, and then I noticed that he said, "Free consultation." So I filled out the form.

He wrote back the next day. He said, "Hi, Joe. How can I help you?" I wrote back and gave him a synopsis of what I was going through. He replied, "The first session is free so you can get a sense of who I am. You can ask all the questions you like."

I was so sold that I wrote back and said, "I don't need a free session. I'm ready. Let's just book the session." I got on the phone with him. We did a session.

In the first twenty minutes, exploring my grief about my father, Dr. Mau gave me some answers that still give me strength. Then he did a twenty-minute hypnosis session with me. He sent me the audio recording, so I can keep listening to it to relax and reinforce the messages he gave me.

All of this is to illustrate how to find the mentor or coach that you want to hire. I wanted a result that was escaping me, even with all the clearing techniques I know. Since, of course, one of these techniques is to get a coach, I knew that that was what I needed right now.

Then I thought, "Whom do I get? Well, I'm reading a couple books by this guy." Books give credibility; books give a person authority. That moved me in the direction of thinking he was the person.

Then I looked at his website. I saw whom he had worked with before. I saw his credentials; I saw his experience. Then I saw that I could have a free conversation with him.

This an example of what you can do, not necessarily with Dr. Mau, but with any coach you're curious about.

Some people wonder whether you need to pay a professional coach or whether you can have a friend, family member, or associate act as your coach.

This is where I have to get in your face. You have money. You are choosing to use it for certain things. I know you have to pay your rent and light bill, but you have other money that you're wasting, you are just using it for some sort of shopping. Coaching and mentoring are going to be the most valuable investments in your life and your own career.

One of my favorite stories is about Jen Sincero. Jen Sincero was struggling. She was broke. She was uncertain. She heard about coaching, called up a coach, and told her life story.

The coach said, "You need to hire me as your coach, and I'll start training you." The coach wanted $5,000. Jen panicked. She had no money and no income: she would have to put that money on her credit card. After a sleepless night, she decided to go ahead and put it on the credit card.

Then she freaked out and ran to the bathroom to throw up. She thought, "This is all the money in the world. How am I going to pay this? This is the dumb-est mistake of my life. I'm investing in this coach. I don't know who she is; I don't know what kind of results I'm going to get. All I know is I'm out $5,000."

She called the coach to ask for the money back, but the coach said, "I'm not giving you the money back. What you're going through is part of the process. Stay with it."

Jen did. Today Jen Sincero is the author of three *New York Times* best-selling books. The first was *You Are a Badass*. I found it in a bookstore, read it, and thought, "This is a fantastic book." I reached out to Jen and inter-viewed her, which is why I know the inside story. We had lunch when she came to Austin, and I heard about the sec-ond book. It's called *You Are a Badass at Money*. All of this came from Jen going through coaching and finding her own inner gems. Coaching helped her to have the confi-dence to step forward and write her books, not knowing what would happen. She didn't think they'd become best sellers. For her second book, she received an advance of $2 million.

There's a funny story behind that book. She had put together a proposal for it and then went overseas to go biking with a friend. There was a publisher who wanted the book, and they made an offer of $1 million, but Jen didn't see it because she was biking overseas. By the time she got to see the offer, the publisher was freaking out, thinking, "We're not giving enough money." They dou-bled it, so that when she finally heard the offer, it was $2 million. All of this from a woman who was collapsing because she was spending $5,000 on a credit card.

Yes, you need to pay, because it shows your commitment to change. You don't want to go to a friend who is not skilled. You don't want to go to somebody who is not going to charge you, because a coach is exchanging time and energy and expertise. You are paying for something you are getting. When you are paying, you are telling your own body and mind that you are committed, and you are in for the long haul. You want this result so badly that you're putting your money on the table.

What's the difference between a therapist and a coach? Usually when we look for a coach, we're looking for a specific, tangible, outer-world result. I did mention my grief, and dealing with grief is probably more in the range of psychological counseling. Dr. Mau is a therapist himself and a hypnotist, so I made the right decision there.

Let me give a different example. A few years ago, I was asked to speak at a big event, for 20,000 people, in Lima, Peru. I was going to be on stage where KISS had performed the week before, so I knew that this was a huge event, but I also knew that if I could speak even a little Spanish I would really win that crowd.

I hired a coach to help me learn Spanish. To do this, I had to get through my own limitations, because I had taken Spanish in high school, when I was insecure, quiet, and shy, and I didn't feel that I had the talent to learn it.

Decades later, I still had those limiting beliefs. In this case, I had to hire a coach to get a specific result. I did not go to a counselor or a therapist, because for this particular result I didn't need one. With grief, on the other hand, going to a psychologist is probably the appropriate thing to do.

In short, you need to ask, what result do I want? If you want to have a new relationship but are dealing with severe abuse from childhood, maybe you want to have a psychologist or psychiatrist instead of a traditional coach. Are you looking to increase your business? In that case, you probably don't need a psychiatrist: this is a matter of who's going to help move you forward to get results in your business. But if you have an ailment stemming from a tragedy, you might need psychological or psychiatric help. There's nothing bad in that. It's just a different kind of coaching.

In regard to coaching, here's what I recommend that you do, step by step. The first is, what is the result that you want? Write it down.

The second is, who can help you achieve that result? You can do a Google search. Depending on what you want, you might search for a counselor or for a mentor or coach. My own coaching company is called Miracles Coaching. It's at miraclescoaching.com. You can review the site and fill out a form. You'll get a phone call. You can find out if it's a match for you.

When you do get the match, whether it is from Miracles Coaching or from your Google search, look at the biography of this person. Where did they get their training? What are they specializing in?

Then look at the testimonials. How long has this person been doing this? What case studies can they can tell you about? Have they written anything? Do they have a blog? Do they have books?

The next thing is actually to interview them. You are interviewing coaches to find an appropriate one for you.

The final step would be to pick one—put your money where your mouth is, like Jen Sincero—and then expect miracles. This is the mind-set I want you to have as you read this book.

Chapter Nine

The Sixth
Clearing Technique:
Tapping and EFT

have been using tapping for decades. I first learned about it from Roger Callahan, who created Thought Field Therapy, or TFT. At that time, decades ago, TFT was all over the airwaves. Roger Callahan was doing major television shows. He'd have people come on who were afraid of ladders. He'd do TFT, and five minutes later, they were going up a ladder. Or he'd have somebody who was afraid of spiders; five minutes after TFT, they were playing with them.

At that time I was suffering from stage fright. I didn't want to go on stage as a speaker; I'd grown up shy and introverted and insecure. Then I heard about EFT. There was an ad in an airline magazine that said, "Fear of public speaking? Handle it in five minutes."

"Give me a break," I thought. "Handle it in five minutes? This is a lifetime problem."

Tapping is a form of psychological acupuncture: you're tapping on specific points on your body in order to release energy blocks. Acupuncture has been around for at least 5,000 years. There's a great deal of research proving that it does work. I've done many acupuncture sessions myself when I've had physical pains, and I've always had a breakthrough. It's always made a difference in my life.

Traditional acupuncture uses needles to go just barely past the surface skin at certain specific points to release energy blocks there. The theory is that when you release these energy blocks, energy moves through your body. What was blocked is now unblocked, and you feel better. With psychological acupuncture, instead of using needles on those spots, you tap them with your fingers.

I first learned TFT from Roger Callahan, who has since passed on. His wife still teaches it. Today people are using it in a lot of different ways. I have a program with Brad Yates called "Money beyond Belief." We use tapping to help people get more money.

A variant is called EFT, which is Emotional Freedom Techniques. A lot of people are teaching it. One of my favorites is Nick Ortner. He came out with a movie, originally entitled *Try It on Everything*, although he later renamed it *The Tapping Solution*. He also has a book called *The Tapping Solution*; now there is even an app called the Tapping Solution.

I use EFT virtually every day. I think about the result I want, and then I think about whether I am in alignment with it. Is there a block within me? Is there a belief that's holding me back? If I can name it, I then tap on it.

Different EFT practitioners have different approaches to tapping. Mine is very simple and abbreviated, and that's what I'm going to be sharing in this chapter, because I've seen it work. You can use it on anything that's going on. If you get more interested, there's even a book called *The Science behind Tapping*. You can dig into the research, which shows that you can use tapping on virtually anything—a physical problem, a psychological problem.

Nick Ortner's movie shows people who have been in car accidents, who have lost loved ones, who are going through things that are so hard and so big that you wouldn't imagine that tapping could handle them. Yet it does. That's why was the original title was *Try It on Everything*. I don't care what's going on in your life. Try tapping on it. See if it makes a difference.

In essence, you are tapping on your hand, your head, your face, or sometimes your upper body to remove a block to getting the results you want.

Let me quickly walk through how I do tapping. This is the Dr. Joe approach.

I think about what's blocking me. I've mentioned public speaking, and I still get nervous before I speak, especially if it's a gigantic audience. I've been on *Larry King* a couple times. Although you don't see the people watching, when the red dot goes on, you know one million people are now watching you sneeze or blink or cough or stutter. Knowing that before I go on, I might have some nervousness about it.

I take whatever is bothering me, and I try to condense it to one or two words. In this case, we'll say "nervous." I then take my left hand. It's open, and I tap underneath what I call the karate spot of my hand. I'd be using this part under the palm to do a karate move or break a brick.

I tap this spot fairly hard with two fingers of my other hand and say. "Even though I feel nervous"—I plug in the word or phrase for whatever is bothering me—"even though I feel nervous, I deeply love, accept, and forgive myself." I tap hard enough to knock on a door or a table.

As I tap this part of my left hand, I say, "Even though I feel nervous, I deeply love, accept, and forgive myself." I say it three times. "Even though I feel nervous, I deeply love, accept, and forgive myself." Sometimes just saying that gives me relief, but I don't stop there.

I take the word that I'm trying to clear: in this case, it's "nervous." I then go to the top of my head, right on the top of my skull, what some people would call the crown chakra. I tap that area and say, "Nervous. Nervous." I take the word that I'm trying to release, I repeat it, and I tap it two or three times: "Nervous. Nervous. Nervous."

Next I go to the place right above the inner eyebrows. I tap the same way. I say, "Nervous. Nervous. Nervous," and I'm tapping pretty hard.

Then I go to the outside of my eyes on both sides of my face. I tap there and say, "Nervous. Nervous. Nervous." Then I go under my eyes and tap, "Nervous. Nervous. Nervous." I repeat it three times.

I go to the philtrum, the little cleft above your mouth and under your nose, and I say, "Nervous. Nervous. Nervous." Then I go under the lip, to the little dent right above the chin, and tap, "Nervous. Nervous. Nervous."

I go right under the left collarbone; right under there is a little soft spot. I rub it and I say, "Nervous. Nervous. Nervous."

By then, "nervous" is usually gone. But if I feel like it, I'll go all the way back to where I started.

This is a very abbreviated version. The Tapping Solution app has a variety of other ways to do tapping. For a very small investment, you can go there, pick what you're trying to take care of—insomnia, pain, frustration, grief, virtually everything you can think of. You pick the issue, and there is a video that will walk you through what to do, how to do it, and what to say, but what I'm giving you above is all you really need.

In the movie *The Tapping Solution*, I teach this version of tapping. That movie came out a number of years ago. Since then people have been using what they have learned and are running down the road with it. They're get fantastic results.

Since this book is about results, let's say you're not getting a particular result, and it's frustrating you. The first thing you do is look for what describes what you're feeling; it could be "frustration."

You could be feeling, "I'm trying everything, and my business isn't blossoming," or, "I am dating, and I'm not finding my soul mate," or, "I'm trying to heal this particular problem, and I'm not getting it healed." What comes up for you as the emotion? Whatever it is, you put a word or phrase on it: "frustration" or "I am very frustrated by this." Then I tap it away, using the technique I've just described. "Even though I feel"—put in the word—"*frustrated*, I deeply love, accept, and forgive myself." This is very important, because saying, "I deeply love, accept, and forgive myself" rebuilds enthusiasm for your well-being and your self-respect.

Some people ask, "When you're tapping the word, aren't you tapping it in?" Actually it's the opposite. You're tapping it out. You're taking what you're being bothered by—"even though I feel frustrated"—and tapping it out. "I deeply love, accept, and forgive myself."

I usually only have to do the tapping once, but a lot of people will do rounds of it. A woman in Thailand was suffering from terrible illnesses that were keeping her in pain all the time. She did tapping all day long. She was bedridden, so her alternatives were to wallow in the pain or to try to do something about it.

Today she is pain-free. In fact, the last time I went to Thailand, I brought her on stage; she spoke about tapping and walked everybody through the process. Later I found that one of her long-standing dreams was to be on stage with Dr. Joe.

So people tap for physical problems, for psychological problems. When you come across things that are keeping you from getting your desired result—a mind-set, a belief, an emotion—you can tap it away quickly and easily with this method.

Emotions are created by people's thoughts. If, for example, you feel frustrated, there is a belief under the frustration that's creating it. The trigger for the emotion is the deeper statement or belief. Instead of just trying to release the emotion, we want to release the trigger for the emotion.

Let's take the belief "I never have enough money." That belief is causing you to feel a certain way—angry, frustrated, embarrassed, guilty. There may be any number of other emotions, but they are created by that belief. So we work with the belief.

I would raise my left hand and open it up. I'd have that karate part of my hand open at the bottom. I'd start tapping it and say, "Even though I feel like I never have enough money, I deeply love, accept, and forgive myself." I'm tapping the whole time I'm saying this: "Even though I feel like there isn't enough money, I deeply love, accept, and forgive myself." I do that three times.

Then I'd take either the whole statement or a condensed version of it, such as "Not enough money," and I'd go to the top of my head—"Not enough money"—and I would tap. "Not enough money." I'd go to the inside of the eyebrows, on the top side of the eyes, saying, "Not enough money."

Underneath the eyes: "Not enough money." Underneath the nose: "Not enough money." Underneath the chin: "Not enough money." Under the collarbone: "Not enough money." I would then come back under my hand and say, "Even though I believe there's not enough money, I deeply love, accept, and forgive myself."

One round of that may release it. There's nothing wrong with doing two or three rounds. I did a mastermind group once in which one fellow was a specialist in tapping. At dinner, we talked about different ways of tapping, and this man demonstrated how he did it, which was very similar to what I do, except that he would tap seven or eight times on an issue or a belief to be sure it was gone. That was a learning experience for me, because I've usually thought that I just needed to do it once. Often you only have to do it once, but don't be afraid to do it a handful of times.

How is it possible that tapping a few points on the body could reprogram us emotionally and attitudinally? Some people might ask, "What is that tapping doing, and why in those specific places? Isn't this just a placebo effect?"

First of all, I love the placebo. It's all based on what we believe anyway. We're living in a make-believe universe. Many facts point to the conclusion that the placebo rules our lives. I love Dr. Joe Dispenza's book *You Are the Placebo*. The placebo is powerful.

There are actually studies of people who had bad knees. They were told they were going to get knee surgery, were wheeled in the operating room, and had a little incision made in their knee to give them the feeling that they had surgery. Then they were wheeled out. They never had the actual surgery, but they got better. They acted as if they had knee surgery. It was a placebo, which tells us that the mind is incredibly powerful. We can create things. We can have things. We can heal things. We can get the results we want if we believe it.

Fake surgeries, and the people feel better? I don't know how they can do this ethically, but those stories are real, and they're in books like Dr. Joe Dispenza's.

I would not put down the placebo. If tapping is working because you believe in it, then by God, just keep doing it. It's working.

The second thing is I would tap on disbelief. I would take the phrase, and tap on it: "Even though I don't believe this works, I deeply love, accept, and forgive myself. Even though I believe tapping is BS, I deeply love, accept, and forgive myself. Even though there's not a chance in hell that tapping is going to work for me, I deeply love, accept, and forgive myself."

Then I'd take one of those phrases, or the shorthand version, go to the top of my head, and say, "Tapping is crap. Tapping is BS." Go to the side of my eyes, "Tapping doesn't work." Underneath my eyes, "Tapping is stupid." Underneath my nose, "Tapping is a joke." Underneath my lip, "Tapping is a fool's game." Underneath my collarbone, "Tapping is a joke." Back to my hand, "Even though I don't believe tapping works, I deeply love, accept, and forgive myself." You can tap away your own skepticism using your skepticism as the starting point.

Finally, this book is presenting a buffet. You walk up, and you scan what's here, and if you find something that appeals to your appetite, go there. If tapping isn't doing it for you, skip tapping for now. Try it another time.

For me and for tens of thousands of other people, it's the greatest free tool we can think of, but if it doesn't work for you, or you don't feel it does, go to the next buffet item.

CHAPTER TEN

The Seventh Clearing Technique: Rewriting Your Story

You may think, "My past is concrete. My past is factual. My past is unchangeable," but those beliefs are illusory.

New research in psychology shows that we don't remember anything correctly. There have been many stories of people having phantom memories that, when investigated, are discovered never to have taken place. Maybe the person saw a movie, or had a dream, and remembered it as real. Maybe their brain manufactured it altogether. In any event, we don't remember facts or specifics with any degree of accuracy.

Certainly we don't see our past accurately. We see it through the lens of today—our perceptions, our paradigm, our mind-set, our beliefs. When people look back and say, "I had a terrible childhood," that is a judgment and a belief and a perception about what took place.

Leo Buscaglia, the late author and inspirational teacher, was a wonderful, endearing, spiritual warrior of the light. Decades ago I got to meet him. I stood in line for two hours. Why did it take two hours? Because he took forever with each person. He sat with each person and talked to them.

I read an interview with Leo in which he said his childhood was wonderful. Then they interviewed his brother, who said, "I don't know what he's talking about. Our childhood was miserable. We struggled, we starved, we were unhappy." The brother looked at the same situation, the same set of facts, and he said, "Man, that was bad." Leo looks at the same situation, the same background, the same family, and he says, "It was heaven. It was so great." Which was true? They were both true.

As I've already said, life is an optical illusion. You see what you believe, so we have to stop and ask whether we're looking at our past in a way that serves us. Is it helping us get the results we want or not?

Many people are still coming from the victimhood stage, especially when they look at their family and upbringing. They think, "Oh, if it was different! If my parents had said this or done this or been this, or if this event had actually taken place . . ."

We all look for the moment like the one in the movie *Back to the Future,* where the father goes back in time and relives a moment. This time, instead of being bullied by the bully, he hits the bully, which creates a whole new future timeline for him. He becomes a strong and successful family man and science-fiction author, all because his past was changed.

I love this movie because it illustrates this particular clearing technique. We look at our past and say, "I can understand that it might have taken place that way, which may or may not be factual. How would I prefer it to be?" We sit down and write a new story. We write a new script.

I remember doing this for the first time in my life. I was still struggling, I was still unpublished, I was still unknown, but I was working on myself, and I was scrambling to learn clearing techniques so I could get more results. I wanted to be an author.

I blamed many of my current struggles on my past. I would say to myself, "If my father had taught me about prosperity, or if he had encouraged my writing, or if my mother had encouraged me to be an author early on, or if they didn't have all of these hang-ups about deserving wealth and success, I wouldn't have my hang-ups."

I blamed my parents—which is victimhood—and then I thought, "I keep hearing about writing another story. How can I reinterpret the past? How can I go back and pretend it actually happened a different way?"

So I sat down, took a pen and paper, and wrote, "I was born in a happy family. My father had a great attitude about wealth: he did work hard for a living, and he earned his money honestly, but he also understood there was more than enough to go around. He had an abundance mind-set. My mother read books to me when I was a child"—which in fact she did—"but she also encouraged me to write my own books early on. I started to write when I was just a child. I would go in the bedroom, I'd close the door, and I'd start to write a short story. When I came out and shared it with my folks, they would encourage me. They would applaud it. They would find the good in it."

I'm making up all of this. I'm rewriting the story of my past. Since I'm not remembering the past accurately anyway, let me create it the way I would like to remember it.

How you view things is how you create things. How I view my past is influencing my present and my future. If I create a new, more empowered story, I can create a new, empowered moment; out of that, I can create a new result in the future.

Byron Katie, one of my favorite spiritual leaders, often asks, "Who would you be without your story?" Your story is the story you're telling yourself right now, and you can rewrite it.

There are people who blame their genes. "I have weight genes," or, "I have bad personality genes. I have anxiety genes." Stephen Covey, author of *The Seven Habits of Highly Successful People*, would say, "Your genes may influence you, but they don't have to determine you."

The same is true with your past. Circumstances influence you, but you are bigger than your circumstances. Bruce Lipton's book *The Biology of Belief* discusses scientific evidence that your genes can be turned on and turned off by your thoughts, beliefs, and emotions. Lipton says your genes are almost suggestions: you fuel them with your own attention, belief, emotion, and energy. Somebody who is pessimistic tends to turn off the life force. An optimistic person tends to turn on the life force.

This idea is so empowering, so freeing. You can look at your past and say, "It may not have been ideal, but I am bigger than those circumstances."

Let me digress here to make an important point. Sometimes people read inspirational books, go to seminars, and so on, but they don't make the changes they want. This is for one key reason: they return to their environment and fall into their old ways of being, thinking, and doing, because their environment—what's around them—reminds them of their old selves.

If you have gotten this far in this book, you've made internal changes. You've stated results you want, and you've started to clear in order to get those results. What can you do to anchor this change, to really make it happen?

Change the environment in your home or office. Move the desk. Move the furniture. Put up a painting. Paint the walls. Move if you need to, but do something that signifies, "I have made a change." This is a missing secret to lasting change that most people don't talk about.

At the end of a long presentation, I will tell people, "You've been fed inspiration, you've been fed information, but when you go home, you will tend to fall into your old habits and routines unless you do one thing: change your environment."

This doesn't mean get up and move to another city, but it does mean to do something in the house that shows you're different. I'm a guitar collector, so I will buy a guitar when I've had a breakthrough; it anchors the moment. I have a caricature made and signed by Mark Twain, which I bought after I had a success. I put it on my desk; it anchors my success and reminds me of it. These things don't have to be big. You can buy a new pair of shoes, and every time you put them on, it's a reminder that you're now Superwoman or Superman because you've made this internal change.

In short, rewrite your story and anchor the change by changing something in your environment to remind you of that transformation.

Your story is a narrative, and everyone has a narrative that they tell. Like any great novel, you can write that narrative as a happy tale with a happy ending. Others have chosen to write the narrative of their lives as a tragedy: "I was born on the wrong side of the tracks. I never had any of the breaks. I've had one thing after another happen to me. This person left me." Their narrative is one of tragedy. For others, it might be more of a mystery novel.

In the narrative of our lives, we can change the meaning of characters, events, and plotlines and write a more empowering narrative to enable us to get the results we want. It's almost like looking at your life like a novel. What story are you recounting to people you meet? Is it a comedy, a tragedy, a mystery, a whodunit?

We are storied beings. We make sense of our lives with the stories we tell. When we communicate to other people, we communicate in the form of stories. They understand our lives and their own lives through stories. How we tell our story is going to influence how we feel and the results we get.

Look at the story you tell: does it serve you in getting results or not? When I was homeless, I believed that my life had to be adventurous, desperate, and melancholy, like Jack London's or Ernest Hemingway's. Was that helping me get the result I wanted? No. It was leading me down the drain, into mental torture and anguish. I had to tell a different story.

Which new story? Surely, I reasoned, there are authors who are happy, healthy productive, and popular. I decided to find those authors and model them, I created a new story for myself—a story I am still writing today.

You have a story. You're midway through it. You have a long way to go here. It's like writing a movie; right now, you are in the movie of your life. You can change the direction of this movie right now. You can change the nature of your story right now. Maybe up to this moment, it's been a story of struggle, of wrestling with life. But now you know how to set new goals and new results. Now you know half a dozen techniques or more for getting clear of the things that used to block you. Now it's becoming the hero's journey.

My father used to tell this story over and over again, and we all laughed every time he told it. He said that when he was young, he went to a psychic. He wanted to know about his future, and the psychic said, "Up to the age of forty, you are going to struggle. You're going to have a hard time. You're going to be broke almost all the time. You're going to struggle with money."

"Great," he said. "What happens after the age of forty?"

"You'll get used to it."

Those who don't know the material I'm presenting in this book might subscribe to the belief that you just have to get used to the struggle, but we're writing a new story here. This story says the struggle is over. You never have to struggle again.

Mike Dooley, who has the website tut.com (for "think unique thoughts"), sends out a note from the universe every morning. Years ago, he sent one out that said, "Would you like to never have to worry about money again?" He added, "OK, wish granted. You never have to worry about money again."

The reality is you don't have to worry about money. It's not serving you. Same thing with struggle. You don't have to struggle anymore. It doesn't serve you.

Write a new story. Write it out the way you would like it to be, flesh out the feelings, the emotions, the characters. Realize that the story you've been telling yourself can be rewritten, and the story you tell about your future can be retold right now.

Of course you can rewrite your past, but your future is unscripted and unwritten. You can sit here and write out how you would like it to be.

A hard-core skeptic might think, "What good is it going to do if I say that I'm in the Fortune 500, and I'm making up all this stuff that's not going to come true?"

Here's the thing: you don't know what's going to come true or not. When you script out how you would like it to be, you're giving orders to your mind to go in that direction.

Your mind doesn't know the difference between reality and imagined reality. When you sit down and draft how you would like the future to be, using what the reticular activating system likes—imagery, emotion, and repetition—you reprogram that system to bring this new experience into being.

Why? Because in a way you've tricked your own mind. Since your mind doesn't know that what you just scripted is imaginary, it looks at it as real. It will begin to go about making it real for you.

A few nights ago, I had a nightmare, and when I woke up, my body was sweating, I was uptight, and I felt as if it had actually happened, although it hadn't. My mind was tricked. My mind felt as if there was a python with a face on it, and it was coming after me. My mind looked at that as if it were real and responded physiologically as if it were real.

This is what happens when you script your future. Your mind is taking it as real. It then moves you in the direction of making it happen. Now you still are cocreating your reality. You still have to take action. You still have to act on opportunities that come to you, but your mind, being part of the universal mind, is bringing you into a situation where it can make that future story actually manifest.

How do you write this story? First of all, we can all write. We can write notes to ourselves. We write emails. We write narratives. We may not think of ourselves as authors, but you don't need to be, not for the purposes of this exercise.

Let's make this as simple as possible. First, you're only writing for yourself. You don't have to share it. Maybe you'll want to at some point, but for now it's personal; it's yours. Mistakes are OK. Misspellings are OK. Fragmented sentences are OK. You're not going to be graded on this.

This is your own personal magic wand to create your imagined future and bring it into reality. I recommend writing it to a person you've never met. Imagine that you're writing to Sue in North Dakota or Tom in Pennsylvania. You're never going to meet Sue or Tom, but it will help you to focus on what you're writing. You'll have more rapport and ease if you imagine writing it to a stranger. You don't want to write it to a friend, because you'll imagine what the friend already knows, but if a stranger doesn't know anything, you'll be inclined to be more revealing.

Then write the story. In this particular case, write your future. Tell me how your future played out, and tell me the good stuff. Tell me the way you wanted it to go and how it did go.

If you are an author, and you want to be on *The New York Times* best-seller list, say, "I woke up this morning. I looked at *The New York Times*, and my book was number one on the list. I clipped it out, and I'm putting it on the wall so I can see it every day. In fact, I'll send a clipping of it when I send this to you."

Say a woman wants to open a bakery. She writes, "I finally opened my business. I just woke up one morning, and I decided today was the day. I went online, and I found that the website name I had in mind, Gluten-Free Yummy Cakes by Betty, was available, and I got it. I'm taking photos of my products, and I'm putting them online. In fact, you can go to this website and see them now."

Write your successes as if they've happened today or very recently. If you've been wanting to work out, you might write, "I've been now going to the gym for three months. It has become a habit. I look forward to it. I found the exercise that I love doing. When I look in the mirror, I'm proud of myself. The other day I was walking down the street, and my jeans were so loose that I knew I needed to get new ones."

Somebody looking for a relationship might write a story that says, "Last night was one of the greatest nights of my life. It was my seventh date with this person. We have so much in common. I can't believe I've finally found my soul mate. We're announcing our engagement, and here's the date and time for the wedding."

Pick the result you want, imagine it's either fulfilled or about to be fulfilled, and write a short, joyous, celebratory description of it. Put in all the smiley-faced stuff, the good-feeling stuff, the Glad Game stuff, so that when you reread it, you feel that this is happening or has happened.

This is a way to create your future, to get a result that you haven't had yet. Again, you're tricking your mind. Your mind's going to look at this story much like a nightmare in which you think, "This feels real." Your mind's going to say, "This feels real. Let's make it happen." That's how simple it can be.

Remember that the reticular activating system is the part of your mind that creates your reality. You program it with emotion. You do not create without emotion. Most people focus on hate, on fear. We don't want to focus on that. We want to focus on love. So imagine the good qualities. Fuel this with desire. Fuel this with fun. Fuel this with love.

The reticular activating system also responds to imagery. Describe what's going on, what you're wearing, what the other person is wearing, the weather, the place. Make it rich in sensory detail so that when you reread it, you can see it, feel it, sense it.

The reticular activating system also responds to repetition. Reread or rewrite your little scenario whenever you feel like it, whenever it's exciting for you, because repetition constantly puts it into the mind as a new program. I would suggest that you read it in the morning, and don't just read it, but actually visualize it. Feel it. Get into imagining that it's already real for you. I'd do the same thing in the evening, because these are prime-time periods to access them.

Occasionally, rewrite the story; elaborate on it; enrich it. If you've been looking at your writing in the morning and the evening for a week and suddenly you realize, "Wow, I'd really like to have this additional experience," or, "I have some new ideas," rewrite it again.

Those three things—emotion, imagery, repetition—inserted in your writing can help create a new result in your future.

As for length, I don't want this to turn into work, because part of what's going to drive the manifestation of a new result is the thrill of doing it. If I said to write fifteen pages, it would to feel like drudgery; you're going to dread even trying it. Instead, just write a couple of paragraphs or a page or two. If you get carried away, keep writing, but only write for as long as it's joyful for you, because joy is an emotion, which activates the reticular activating system. As long as it's fun, as long as it's joyful, feed that emotion to the result you want.

CHAPTER ELEVEN

The Eighth Clearing Technique: Nevillizing

This eighth clearing technique, *nevillizing*, is a term that I coined. It's named after Neville Goddard, an inspirational teacher who was active from the 1940s to the 1970s and who influenced a long line of people. He usually went by just Neville, and signed and autographed his books "Neville." He died in 1972. Today he is very popular. Many of his books and talks are being republished. I myself republished his first book some fifteen or twenty years ago: *At Your Command*—a long-lost book, but a classic. The title is suggesting that the world is at your command: you can have the result you want by commanding it.

Neville often talked about creating your own reality by doing something that's beyond what most people do, and that's what I want to talk about in this chapter. Most people, when they decide to create a result, know about the power of visualization: you visualize that you have the result or are about to get it. We know visualization works; it's been scientifically proven. It influences the mind, it influences the body.

Neville did something different. He said instead of visualizing what you want to have, do, or be, you sit here in this moment, and you imagine it has *already* come true, yesterday or this morning. Instead of pushing the result off in the distance, which is what a lot of people do when they imagine or visualize, Neville says to imagine it took place today.

I have a couple of books autographed by Neville; in one of them he wrote, "Assumption hardens into fact." When you assume that an event is going to take place, your assumption will take hold in your mind, and through a mystical process—Neville was very much a mystic—it will harden into concrete, objective reality. In another book he wrote, "Assume the feeling of the wish fulfilled."

What does that mean? The wish is the result you want. "Assume the feeling of the wish fulfilled" means, what would it feel like emotionally, internally, in your body and in your mind once your result has been fulfilled? Assume the emotional state that you would have if your result had already manifested at this moment.

It goes back to what I discussed in the previous chapter. Neville knew that if you could visualize what you wanted as if it has already the place, a part of you believes that it's already real. A part of you believes that this is how it's going to be, and you react as if it's reality.

With nevillizing, you're creating the result you want now using mental imagery and a kind of self-hypnosis. You're tricking yourself into believing the result has already taken place.

Sometimes people will ask me about a car they want to attract. They'll tell me it's a Mercedes or something. I'll say, "All right. Imagine that you already have the car. You went for a drive in it this morning. You're going to pick me up later. We're going out to dinner, and you're going to take me for a drive in your car, and the keys are in your wallet or in your desk drawer at this very moment. What does that feel like?"

Move into this imaginary experience of pretending it's already real is what I call *nevillizing*. You're taking Neville's concept—"assume the feeling of the wish fulfilled"—and you are turning it into a clearing tool to get a result.

This works because it takes away the excuses, the doubts, the skepticism. The only way for you to assume the feeling of the wish fulfilled is to assume that it has already happened. To do this and to step into the reality of this manifestation means your doubts and concerns are gone. There is an underlying assumption that it must have worked, that it must have taken place. This is exciting. This is a breakthrough.

Let's say I'm starting a new business. Instead of visualizing the steps I need to take to leave my current job, get financing, and so on, I'm imagining that the business is up and running. I see myself running the business, shipping products, seeing the looks on employees' faces.

This leads to something I want to get across to everybody. I gave a talk recently, and somebody asked, "What is the biggest mistake people make when they go for their results?"

I'll tell you what it is. *It's needing to know how.* I understand the feeling, because you're sitting there, thinking, "I want to get to the end result, but I'm sitting here at the starting line, and I don't know how to get there. How do I do that?" We all look for the how-to. We all look for the plan.

Here's what I want everybody to get: *there is no plan.* There is no plan when you begin. Steve Jobs said, "You cannot connect the dots looking forward. You can only connect the dots looking backwards."

When you're at the start and you ask, "How am I going to get there?" there are no dots to connect. When you get to your end result, you can turn around, look back, and say, "That was step one, that was step two; that dot led to that dot," and you can tell the story, but in the beginning you don't have that map.

In fact, if somebody said, "Here's the roadmap. Here is step 1, and here's step 32. Do all of these 32 steps, and you'll get there," you won't get there with that map, because the map is not the territory. You are creating your result out of a moving time period—people, technology, everything is in flux. What you think is going to work, or what worked ten or twenty years ago, isn't necessarily going to work now, because everything has changed. We're in a different moment. You have to respond to the moment.

The big problem is thinking, "I need to know the map now. I need to know all the steps." You do not. You only need to know one thing, the first step, what I often call the baby step. That's the one you take. It could be buying a book. Getting a domain name. Attending seminar. Phoning somebody. Daydreaming. Doing one of the clearing techniques.

Whatever that baby step is, it's apparent in this moment. If you do that step, guess what? The next step becomes apparent. You don't get to see all the steps in advance. You have to take the first, baby step, then the second step becomes apparent.

The novelist Elmore Leonard said that writing a book is like driving your car across the United States at night. You can only see 100 yards or so in front of you—whatever the headlights show—but once you've made it that far, the next part is illuminated, and then the next part. That's how you manifest your desires.

Nevillizing shows you the target, the end result; it's just not showing you consciously. Think of the submerged part of the iceberg: the unconscious/subconscious mind. Think of the reticular activating system.

You are alerting your brain that this is the result you want to manifest.

Because you are enriching it with emotion, imagery, and repetition, you're programming your mind to look for it. The beauty of nevillizing is it's so much fun. It's thrilling to pretend that the thing you want is already here. Your book is finished. Your bakery is in business. Your business is booming. Your relationship is soaring. The song you wrote is a hit.

You look for the end result, which tells you it is possible; it is real. It's an underlying statement of fact that pulls away all the skepticism, because then you can role-play it: you are scientifically programming your mind to get the result you want.

Nevillizing is mysticism and magic, but it's also a practical tool for getting results. You're turning on your brain to see opportunities that you're otherwise missing. Scientific research that says at any particular moment, there are about fourteen billion bits of information flying by in any moment. That is staggering. We can't even imagine that. Consciously, you can only grasp about seven bits of information. So what is filtering it? What is filtering out all the billions of bits of information and only giving you the seven things that some part of you says is relevant? What is sorting it is the system that is helping you get results.

One result you want, unconsciously at least, is to survive, so the filtering system is looking through all this data for anything dangerous. If there's something dangerous, it will alert you, and you can do something about it, so this system is trying to keep you alive. That's what your reticular activating system is programmed to do, and it's working. Now you're programming it for new results. You're saying, "I want to do X," and the reticular activating system sorts through those billions of bits of information. If there's something relevant to achieving your result, it alerts you. Now you're conscious of it: maybe you have a sudden thought that says, "You need to do this on the Internet," or, "You need to do a search on Google." Whatever it happens to be, you can now be aware of it and take action on it.

Nevillizing makes this possible. It has programmed your mind to look for a result; because of that programming, your brain is on alert for anything that can help you achieve it. Then it tells you by making this thing conscious in your mind: you get an intuitive hit, you see an opportunity, and you then take action. You're cocreating your reality, and your brain will move you in the direction of your result.

How do you incorporate nevillizing into your daily life? My rule of thumb is to do things as long as they're fun, because fun is one of the energies of creation. It's one of the love energies, one of the manifesting energies. Don't want do it out of a sense of duty; don't make it a discipline that they you don't want to do at all.

Maybe when you go to bed tonight, you think it'd be fun to imagine that you got the new car, the new business, or the new relationship. But if it feels like drudgery, don't do it.

Pay attention to your inner compass. What is telling you to do it; what is telling you not to do it? Honor that. The more you do this practice, the more likely you will accelerate the process, but at the same time, nevillizing for one vivid, emotionally satisfying time will manifest the dreams and get you results you want faster than ever before.

CHAPTER TWELVE

The Ninth
Clearing Technique:
Affirmations

To be candid, I've never been a fan of affirmations. For a long time, I thought they were the weakest tool that anybody could use to change themselves. I also thought they didn't work. I would try different affirmations, and I would think, "That's not working. I'm writing down, 'I now have more money,' but I look around and I don't have more money." I felt that affirmations were like lying to myself.

Once I interviewed Jeffrey Schwartz, a medical doctor who wrote the book *You Are Not Your Brain*. He pointed out that we have 50,000 to 60,000 thoughts a day and that most of them are the same old thoughts. Furthermore, these thoughts are affirmations of a kind, even though most of them are negative. These thoughts, which we keep on repeating over and over again in our minds, keep alive a certain way of thinking and being. In order to interrupt this process, we have to create a new pattern, new neural pathways. We need new thoughts.

Let's do a mindfulness exercise. Begin by noticing that you're thinking, and you're having all kind of thoughts. You're thinking about yourself and what you have to do next. You're thinking about clearing techniques.

Notice that you are having thoughts, but *you are not your thoughts*. You can report on your thoughts, but somehow you are somehow not those thoughts.

This is a big insight. It is a great empowerment to realize that you are not your thoughts. When thoughts rush in to say things like, "I'm not good enough," or, "All the good ones are taken," or, "There's not enough money," or, "I don't have the skills," or, "I'm too old or too young," they're just thoughts. You don't have to buy into them. You can actually separate from them, and, as Dr. Schwartz showed in his book, realize you are not your thoughts.

You can go on. Notice your emotions. Are they happy? Are they sad? Are they grieving? Whatever they happen to be, you can notice that you're not your emotions. You have emotions, you can report on your emotions, you can describe your emotions, but you're not your emotions.

We can go still further. Notice your body. How is it feeling right now? You're sitting, you're standing, you're lying down. Are you comfortable? Any aches and pains? Any spasms? Anything going on? Again, notice that you can report on it, but you're not it.

If you're not your thoughts, you're not your emotions, and you're not your body, who or what are you? This is the part of you that some spiritual traditions call the *witness*. This witness, or observer, is the same in you, the same in me, the same in everybody else. It is the inner spiritual essence that you reach when you get past the thoughts, the feelings, and the body.

We can go further, but for the purposes of this chapter, realize that you are having all these thoughts. You have allowed them to influence you, to either inhibit or bring on the results you want, but you are not your thoughts. Since you are not your thoughts, you can begin to play with the idea, "What kind of thoughts would I like to have? Which ones would be better? Which ones would I prefer?"

Earlier I told the story about the woman who said, "Affirmations don't work for me." That's an affirmation. "Affirmations don't work for me" is an affirmation that affirmations don't work for me. Maybe you would call it a negation rather than an affirmation, but in any event, you are creating your reality with these repeated thoughts. These repeated thoughts are affirmations. And right now, you're getting results, or not getting results, from the affirmations you're telling yourself.

I've learned to begin to tell myself the affirmations I prefer. In the past, I used to say, "None of this works for me." I wanted to change that. I don't want to keep repeating, "None of this works for me," because if I do, I will make it so. It will be a self-fulfilling prophecy. I will make things not work by saying, "It doesn't work for me."

What would be better? A new affirmation. "This material works for me." "These clearing techniques work for me." We want to start picking and choosing our preferences, and we want to start saying them. We want to start thinking them. We want to start writing them. We want to start recording them. We want to feed our mind new programming.

Consider affirmations—indeed all thoughts—as software for the mind. We're reprogramming ourselves with new material.

Let's talk about the elements of a good affirmation. It should be in the present tense. It should be positive. It should be short. It should be personal. It should be stated with emotion and clarity to the extent that if you told them to somebody else, they would understand what you're talking about.

In a previous chapter, I mentioned that I inserted a new belief in my reality that I didn't believe at first: the idea that the more money I spend, the more money I receive. How did I do that? I began with an affirmation: "The more money I spend, the more money I receive."

Now, like with all new affirmations, when you first state it, it doesn't feel true. That's because it's clashing against the old affirmations that are still active in the software of the mind, but as you keep saying it, it becomes more integrated into the software.

Many books out there discuss self-talk. Self-talk is affirmations that you are silently saying in your mind. For most people, they consist of things like, "I'm not good enough" or, "I'm a failure" or, "I'm too old." These are weakening statements.

We want to take control of that process. We want to realize we're not our thoughts; we're not even our brains. We have control of all of this. We can write short, new, personal, present-tense affirmations that at first might not seem believable, although they're preferable to what has been going on in our heads.

Over time, "The more money I spend, the more money I receive," becomes a reality. Over time, "I am more than good enough for success" becomes the new reality.

Again, you want affirmations to be short. You want them to be in the first person. You want them to be declarative. You want them to be easy, because you're talking to your brain as if to a baby. In many ways, you are talking to the child that was you.

People have objections to affirmations. Tony Robbins once said that when you say to the mirror, "I am wealthy beyond belief," and you're looking at your $50,000 in credit-card debt, your mind is saying, "BS, BS, BS." The affirmation isn't accepted because it clashes so much with reality.

Other people will say that affirmations are like fool's gold, because in the end, you have to discipline yourself and accept that success is hard work. It's going to take effort. The reality is yes, you have to set your goals, but you're going to have to burn the midnight oil. When you say affirmations, you're trying to skip those facts, and maybe they're going to make you weaker. If "Oh, I've already accepted this, and I've already achieve this."

Time to get in your face. Time to grab you by the throat, look you in the eye and say, "OK, we have to tell the truth here." The first part of the truth is that your current reality is based on the affirmations you've already told yourself. The reality, the result you have now is directly due to the affirmations you've already told yourself. This is how powerful affirmations are.

We want find out what the limiting beliefs are, rewrite them as positive affirmations, and begin to say them. At first, yes, it's going to feel uncomfortable, and it's going to feel as if you're lying, because you're entering new programming in the software of your mind. At first the mind is going to say, "Not accepting. That doesn't go with the flow. That doesn't go with what's already there," but you keep repeating it, and you will quickly take it on as the new reality.

To answer the second objection: the beliefs that success involves suffering and struggle and the things are themselves limiting beliefs. They are inherent affirmations, or negations, that said, "Going for my dreams or going for my results is going to require struggle." Not necessarily. "Going for my dreams, going for my results is going to require discipline." Not necessarily. "Going for my dreams, going for my results is going to require surrendering some pleasure so that I can have this payoff." Not necessarily.

Again, we live in a belief-driven universe. What's another word for *belief*? *Affirmation*. These affirmations, these statements, these beliefs that we keep telling ourselves are creating our reality. If we think it's going to be a struggle to get our results, most likely it will be. We will create it that way by repeating, "It's going to be a struggle." That's an affirmation.

That affirmation is going to create that reality unless we interrupt it and introduce a new affirmation—something like "I achieve my result easily and effortlessly," or, "I achieve my result out of my passion for what I want." Don't those feel better than "It's going to be a struggle"?

I think it was the Buddha who said, "Life is struggle, but once you accept the struggle, there's no longer a struggle." It's a mind-set. Once you accept that there are certain things to do in order to get the result you want, you kind of shrug and go, "Well, that's what I have to do." It's doesn't mean it's bad. It doesn't mean it's a struggle. It doesn't mean it's dark. It's just the next step.

This is the power of affirmations. Don't dismiss it like my friend who said, "Affirmations don't work." We are using affirmations in our day-to-day conversation. We're using them blindly when we have 60,000 thoughts a day. We're using them when we buy into our own excuses: "I'd really like to act on Dr. Joe's advice, but that works for everybody else. It doesn't work for me." That is an affirmation. "It works for everybody else. It doesn't work for me" is a limiting thought. It's a limiting belief. If you keep repeating it, you are affirming it. If you keep affirming it, you create it as your result.

We want to become aware. We want to become empowered. We want to choose what we think. We want to choose what we believe.

A friend of mine named Mendhi Audlin wrote a book called, *What if It All Goes Right?* The idea is to change your thinking in order to ask a different question. Most people practice what she calls *what-if down thinking.* "What if this doesn't work? What if this program backfires? What if all of these clearing techniques work for everybody but not for me? What if I end up being a failure even though I do all the right things?"

What if, stated negatively, is *what-if down.* It pulls down your energy, your enthusiasm, your optimism, your ability. It blinds your mind to your opportunities, your choices, the ability to have the kind of life you want.

What's the opposite? *What-if up thinking.* What if this works out? What if this program changes your life forever? What if these clearing techniques kill off your negative beliefs once and for all? What if because of any one of these techniques, you finally begin to achieve the results you've been dreaming about?

What-if up thinking makes you stronger, happier, healthier, wealthier, more optimistic. It gives you the power to make choices and to cocreate your reality. It will help you get the results you want.

All of this, again, is dealing with thoughts. You can have what-if down thoughts. You can have what-if up thoughts. The book *What if It All Goes Right?* points you toward positive questions. You can choose.

In practical terms, let's outline a program of affirmations. Here are some recommendations.

I like being balanced, so I would look at all the different areas of life, including finances, social life, interpersonal relationships, health, and spirituality. I recommend that you assess your life and choose ten areas that you would like to work on. Then create at least one affirmation for each of those areas.

It could be "I am now healthy, wealthy, and wise." "I am now in a fulfilling relationship." "I am now earning more than enough money" or, "I am receiving more than enough money doing what I love in business.

Use *I* statements: *I have, I am, I do. I am* statements are probably more powerful than any others: "I am wealthy." "I am loved." "I am successful." "I am healthy." From a hypnotic standpoint, they're very powerful commands. They're also very easy for your mind to understand, and they're also declarations of what you want for a result.

I love *I am* statements. I love writing them down and looking at them. I have friends who have written them on yellow stickies and put them where they're going to see them—on their hands, on the steering wheel, the refrigerator, the bedroom or bathroom mirror.

I'm also a great believer in recording affirmations in your own voice. Today it's very easy to pick up your phone and record ten seconds of affirmations. Then listen to them. Listening to your own voice say them is very powerful. It's easier for your mind to accept it that it's you, and it's also easier to understand. It's your voice, not somebody else's.

Again, repetition is one key to reprogramming the reticular activating system, so it's best to expose yourself to these affirmations several times a day. Do it so it's not work. Put them up on a wall where you could see them or on your phone. Maybe you could have them come up as reminders every hour or so.

The more I can look at these affirmations, the more I can remind myself that this is my new thinking. This is my new way of being. This is the new me. These are the new results that I want. I would have fun. Let this be fun. It's an easy process, fun to do, to create the results you want.

One technique that fits in with affirmations is gratitude. Gratitude changed my life.

Let me tell you a story about a yellow pencil. It's a story that illustrates the power of gratitude. This is a clearing technique that anybody, anywhere can do.

Decades ago, I was in Houston, struggling, broke, unknown, unhappy, miserable, but doing all the right things. I was reading the right books, listening to the right cassettes, listening to free seminars. I was doing whatever I could to work on Joe, because Joe wanted to be an author, but nothing seemed to be happening, and I was aggravated, disappointed, and skeptical.

People kept talking about gratitude: "You have to be grateful. If you're grateful, it will shift everything."

"Yeah," I thought, "I'll be grateful when there's something to be grateful for."

They would say, "No, it doesn't work that way. You have be grateful first, and then you get the stuff that you're grateful for."

"Boy, what a game this is," I thought. "Bring me my published work. Bring me my success. Bring me my money. Bring me my car, my wealth, and then I'll be grateful."

But I kept hearing, "No, it doesn't work like that. You need to practice gratitude."

I was sitting in my room, a little old dump of a room in south Houston. There was no space. It was not comfortable. The toilet was in the same room as my desk.

There was a yellow pencil sitting on the desk. I picked it up, looked at it, and said, "OK, I can be grateful for this. With this I can write a suicide note. I can write some kind of ransom letter. I can write some kind of angry memo to the government or to the president or to newspapers."

Then I went on, "I can write a love song. I can write a love poem. I can write a sonnet. I can write a manifesto. I can write the great American novel. I can write a screenplay."

Suddenly I was starting to change, and I thought, "Holy smokes. I can change the world with this pencil."

I was looking at it, and I was genuinely starting to feel gratitude for it. I started to feel different inside. Then I saw the eraser, and I thought, "Oh my God. This is genius. I can erase the suicide note. I can erase the ransom letter. I can erase the grocery list, or whatever I've written that I don't want on the list." I thought, "It's a twig. It's a stick with lead in it and a piece of rubber on the other end, but with it I can change the world."

Every time I tell this story, my energy changes, and my enthusiasm for life goes up. Yet when I began that exercise, I didn't believe it. I didn't believe it would work. I didn't believe in gratitude.

I began with skepticism and anger, but I pretended. I said, "What if I could be grateful for the pencil?"

This is my invitation to you is to pick up something. It doesn't have to be the pencil. It could be your pet that's walking by. It could be your loved one. It could be a glass of water.

At first you might skeptically say, "OK, I'll be grateful for this tablet of paper in front of me," but as you start to play with it and make up reasons why you're grateful, you move into gratitude. Then at a certain point, it lodges, and your whole energy changes.

When I did that pencil, I was still in a $200-a-month room. I was still broke. I was still unknown. I was still struggling, but a new optimism arose. The sun rose inside of me, and I began to see possibilities that I didn't see before.

That was the turning point of my life and my career. After that, I started to get published, and then there was the domino effect. I appeared in the movie *The Secret*, which led to many other deals around the world. I can narrate many magical things that took place, but it all began with a pencil; it all began with gratitude. It all began with trying an exercise that I didn't even believe would work.

This is a way to open to the magnificence of the world. You can call it an affirmation of sorts because I was affirming the beauty of life and how I was grateful for my life, but it all began with me practicing, flippantly at first, gratitude.

CHAPTER THIRTEEN

The Final Stages of Awakening: Results from a Spiritual Perspective

Finally, let's look at results from a spiritual perspective. I've already mentioned the Great Something. For me, the Great Something is all that is. It is life, both inside and out. It refers to what Joseph Campbell called the "Great Mystery." It refers to what some people call God; the Divine, the universe. or Gaia. The Muslims say that there are ninety-nine names for God.

We are all part of this power, but it is still greater than all of us. Thinking we are rulers of the earth and we are gods in and of ourselves is the big mistake.

In the Bill Murray movie *Groundhog Day*, the main character says he is God, but he is not *the* God, he is *a* God. That's where I think we're all at. We are all parts of the Great Something, the Great Mystery, and I say the Great Something because we really don't know what that is.

Some people may stamp their feet and say, "I know exactly what that is" and spout their beliefs about it. What I'm talking about is coming from a place beyond beliefs, a place where you tune in to the inner essence of you. In the meditation that I gave, and I said to go beyond your thoughts and your emotions and your body. What's that inner essence?

That inner essence is the Great Something. That inner essence is the same in you and the same in me. I think that's the spirituality we're all looking for. I think it's available to each of us. I think the Great Something is whatever you end up calling it for yourself.

Everybody has to find their own connection and their own path to this Great Something. For one person, it might be music. For another person, it might be art. For somebody else, it might be walking in nature. For somebody else, it might be meditation.

For me, meditation is one of the most direct routes of direct experience. The meditation I do is the one that I've already described, where I say, "Joe, you're not your thoughts." I have thoughts going on right now, but beyond those thoughts there's a witness. I might have feelings, but I'm not my body. I have emotions, but I'm not my emotions. All of this is a meditation to take me to that witness.

The more you can touch that essence, the more you can get close to it, the more you can sense it and feel it in every moment, the freer and the more empowered you will be. It will be easier to get the results you want out of life, because you will have more of a let-go attitude towards it. This is available to all of us if we practice that meditation.

There are many different kinds of meditation out there. Transcendental Meditation, or TM, is very popular. Watching your breathing is another technique: You sit and observe the breath going into your nose. You observe it going into your lungs. You pause and observe it coming out. You can have a very relaxing meditation by watching your breathing.

Many people benefit from going in nature. Earlier I mentioned Andres Pira, the homeless man who became a billionaire. In his book *Homeless to Billionaire*, one of his eighteen principles for achieving great wealth and seizing opportunity is going out in nature.

Andres does extreme sports. He's not afraid to live in a volcano for five days, to parachute out of planes at extreme heights, or to climb mountains that are almost insurmountable. He's thirty-six years old. He's daring, he's athletic, he's charismatic, and that's how he connects. He told me that one of his biggest ideas came when he was walking the trails around Machu Picchu. Being in nature expanded his mind; it enabled him to be close to the Great Something.

Each person has to find their way. Somebody who writes poetry is probably knocking on the door of the Great Something right there. Somebody who is singing and doing it out of their heart is probably talking to God in that moment. Whether it's painting, athletics, writing, reading, meditation, breathing, swimming, walking, skydiving, or traditional meditation, whatever gets you there is what I support.

You may be asking if spiritual results are different from results in other areas of your life. There is a way to get results from the old, traditional, Type A behavior: drive yourself, separate yourself from your family, get a heart attack, but get your result. That's not the behavior I'm talking about. That's not the way to get results that I've talked about in this book.

The way that I'm talking about is almost like an effortless effort. You're taking action to go in the direction of getting a particular result, but you're not addicted or attached to the result. You almost end up enjoying the journey more than getting there. In fact, you'll realize that the great fun, the great adventure, the great energy and enthusiasm of life actually comes from the journey, because once you arrive, you might take a moment to celebrate, but you're going to shrug and go on to the next thing.

Life is that before-you-get-there-experience. That's living. Yes, you want to get a particular result, but enjoy the path there. Enjoy the trek.

Furthermore, it's far healthier not to be attached to an outcome. I wrote a book called *The Attractor Factor*. It was the book that got me into the movie *The Secret*. It talks about five steps for creating your reality.

The first step is know what you *don't* want. Use that as a springboard to get to the second step, which is choose what you *do* want. The third step is get clear. This whole book has been about different ways to get clear. The fourth step is to nevillize your goal: what would it feel like to achieve it?

The fifth step is to let go while taking inspired action. This means letting go of your need for your result to work out in a particular way. In *The Attractor Factor*, I recommend that when you state your result, you add the proviso, "This, or something better."

If you say, "I want to be an independently wealthy woman with my own clothing line," you end with, "This, or something better." This enables your wider connection to the Great Something to provide you with a result that's even better than what you imagined. When you imagine a result, you usually do it from your ego. It's based on what you think it possible, but the Great Something has a wider view of life, and it can see things you haven't even imagined yet.

Inspired action means that you definitely have to take action. I'm an entrepreneur; I know nothing happens unless you actually do something, but the action you take is not necessarily a directive from a book or from somebody else. Sometimes it can be, but it's coming from you. It's an intuitive nudge. It's an inspiration. It's a feeling.

It's a gut instinct that says, "Do this. Go here. Buy that. Invest in this." You take inspired action with the mindset that this or something better is going to happen as a result, but you're not attached to it. Your life is not going to end if it doesn't work out. You have a spiritual feeling of letting go.

Earlier I mentioned four stages of awakening. I've already discussed the first two: victimhood and empowerment. The next two stages are more spiritual in nature.

To recapitulate, the first stage is victimhood. Most people, including me, are born there. We don't want to stay there, but unfortunately a lot of people do.

The next stage is empowerment. If you're fortunate and have read this book so far, you have moved into empowerment. It is a juicy, exciting stage, and you feel wonderful because you're creating the results you want, but there are two more stages.

When you're in empowerment, you feel as if you are the king of the world. You can have, do, or be anything. The world is your oyster. Unfortunately, at some point, something happens to knock you off your pedestal.

Sometimes it's death. When you face a death, you realize you're not in charge of the universe. You are not God. You are not the Great Something. If I were, my father would still be alive. My mother would still be alive. At a certain point you have to surrender.

There are two kinds of surrender. The first is falling back into victimhood. You say, "Man, none of this ever works out. I am vulnerable to life and to everything that life's going to do to bring me to my knees."

The second kind of surrender is to realize, "I'm on my knees, because life is pointing out I'm not in charge so it's a good time to pray." The surrender you make at that point is a surrender to join forces with a higher power. You surrender to the Great Something.

This is where your will and what we'll call the divine will become one. You are joining forces with something more powerful than your ego. In the first stage, your victimhood is saying, "My ego has no power whatsoever," and you remain as a wounded ego. In the second stage, you are empowered, and now your ego is flexing its muscles and saying, "I have control here. I'm going to be Alexander the Great and rule the planet."

Then something knocks you back and you realize, "I have to surrender." Your choice is to surrender back to victimhood or to surrender into the stage of greater awareness and greater power. It's a wonderful place to be.

This is where techniques like ho'oponopono and meditation are very useful, because they're tapping into the Great Something. They are making you ally with the Great Something, so you realize you are not alone.

With this empowerment, with this spiritual army on your side, you can now accomplish greater results than you ever could before. With empowerment, intention is the winning ticket, but when you get to the point of surrender, you look back and say, "Intentions are for wimps," because now your inspiration is better. Inspiration comes from the Great Something. Sometimes it can really be a lightning strike that opens your mind to possibilities you never saw were there.

Surrender is wonderful, but surrender is the third stage. There's still another one. The fourth stage is what I call *awakening*. Awakening is where you and the Great Something become one. Your ego dissolves into the greater energy, into God, to the Divine, the universe, the Great Mystery, the Great Something. At that point, the Great Something is living and breathing through you.

This is the stage that some people might call enlightenment. Some people have glimpses of it, or for a moment, they feel they're one with all that is. That would be called a satori experience, but when it actually locks in, and you have disappeared into the ocean of life, that's called enlightenment or awakening.

Now all of the stages have exit strategies. In other words, when you are a victim, you can read the right book, you can read *The Attractor Factor*, or see the right movie, *The Secret*, and you slide into empowerment; you've exited victimhood. In empowerment, you are enriched, and there are lots of resources, but at some point you need an exit strategy. Maybe it's a book. I wrote the book *Zero Limits* and the follow-up book, *At Zero*, both about ho'oponopono, which point to the fact that there's another stage.

Then, through that book or some experience that was given to you by the Great Something, you slide out of empowerment. Now you're in surrender. What's the exit strategy from surrender? There is nothing that you can willfully do.

Awakening comes by grace. Awakening comes by the Great Something. You can't sit in the stage of surrender and say, "I'm going to make myself awake," because that would be saying, "I, as an ego, am willing to kill the ego so that I can live without my ego." You won't be able to do it.

You can prepare for awakening with meditation. It's been my experience that when people meditate on not being their thoughts, their feelings, or their bodies, and they pay more and more attention to the background observer, they get closer to that observer. At some point there's a pop: everything falls away, and you and the observer are now one. That, again, comes by grace. These are the four stages of awakening.

You can't move yourself into the stage of awakening. Furthermore, evidence shows that enlightenment can come to anybody at any time, with no preparation whatsoever. The most unlikely person could become enlightened just by the grace of the Great Something.

But there are things you can do to prepare for awakening. It's very wise to do the spiritual and psychological work, meaning let's look at our beliefs and find out what limiting beliefs we have. Let's knock them down, let's erase them. Let's use the clearing techniques to remove them so we're free. What are we free to do? Free to receive. Free to receive new insights, new thoughts, new inspirations.

So doing the clearing work is one of the most important things. Meditation can also help you go within, and the more you go within, the closer you'll be to the Great Something. At some point this will open you from within to the experience of awakening.

I think the third thing to do is nevillizing. What would it feel like if you were awakened right now? What would that be like? I'm going to make up a few things, but I suggest that you do your own version of this.

You'd probably not be worried. You'd probably not be stressed. You'd still be in a physical body having a physical experience in this material, three-dimension plane, but you would be less attached to outcomes.

This is why traditional stories of awakened men and women show them laughing. They are smiling, they are at ease, they're taking themselves lightly, they're looking at life without the stress and strain with which somebody that's not awakened looks at life.

So I would say to myself, "If I were awakened, how would I feel? How would I act? Would I be smiling more? Would I be laughing more? Would I be hugging more? Would I be putting my arms around people more? Would I be writing more? What might I be doing?"

Let's use another clearing technique: write your story of enlightenment. What does your awakening look like? Write it out. Nevillize it. Feel it. What does it feel like to be awakened now?

I think all of this moves us in the direction of preparing for something that is miraculous and comes by grace. When you take a spiritual view of life, you gain a sense of ease and detachment. The shiny objects that appealed to you previously aren't so appealing to you anymore. You might still appreciate them and be grateful for them, but you no longer have a drive to possess them.

That in itself makes it easier for you to attract these things, because you no longer have a repelling force in you. Many people fail to realize that when they want something really desperately, they're unconsciously demonstrating a belief about lack: they believe it's really not going to happen. That's why they feel desperate. Because of that feeling of desperation, they inadvertently sabotage their own efforts to get what they want.

When you come from a spiritual standpoint, the desperation is gone. Now you can just appreciate what you have. I wrote a book called *The Awakened Millionaire*. What's an awakened millionaire? An awakened millionaire is somebody who has the spiritual and the material as two sides of the same coin, and they've made peace with it. They can go after money without needing money or being desperate about it, because they have the awakened view that money is just a spiritual force for good. Money is a useful tool to help you achieve your dreams or to fulfill a mission. Their eyes are open to the reality that nothing on the playing field of life is anything to be attached to, but while we're here, we can enjoy the game.

There's more of an attitude that life is a game, and because it's a game, we don't need to have a heart attack. We don't need to be sick. We don't need to be stressed out. We don't need to alienate family and friends. We can still go for what we want, but with ease, detachment, and playfulness. Consequently, the results come faster, and they are more enjoyable and more appreciated.

Now that we're at the end of this book, let me give you some final tips. First, think bigger than you've ever thought before. You read this book because you wanted results. Maybe they were small, mediocre, or even fairly large. Now think gigantic. Stretch your mind almost to the breaking point.

I read books that help me stretch, for example, by Richard Branson—a big thinker who is going for colossal things. I've also read *Moonshots* by Naveen Jain, another person who was homeless at one point, came to this country, didn't speak the language, didn't have connections, didn't know what he was doing, and now is a very successful entrepreneur. He is teaching people to think so big that he wants them to go for a moonshot.

What's a moonshot? It's John F. Kennedy in the 1960s saying, "We're going to the moon? Why? Because we can't do it, so we're going to go ahead and figure out how to do it, and we'll see if there's something we can bring back." Thinking so big that it boggles the mind of other people.

We've talked about results and different ways to get them, but I want to go back. If you really want to use this program in a way that will make a difference in history— personal history and planetary—stop right now, and you say, "What's the biggest dream I can go for?"

Naveen Jain says that if you have a goal, and it doesn't move a billion people, it's not a big enough goal. He wants you to end homelessness. He wants you to end cancer. He wants you to move the needle on history's scale. When I think about that, I get excited, because I'm thinking there are unlimited possibilities.

Once I saw a documentary in which a group of billionaires were interviewed. One of them said, "If you go to a party and you tell somebody what your dream is, and they don't think you're crazy, you haven't thought big enough."

That's the result I want you to start with. What is the result that other people think is nuts? You're going to go for it. Write that down.

Also notice what comes up because what comes up in your mind will be the limiting beliefs like, "This is crazy. How am I going to do this? Where do I get the money to do this? How do I get the resources to do this? Who am I to do this?" Write those down, because those are the limitations that need to be cleared.

The next step is use this book and all of its techniques. Go to the buffet of clearing techniques, pick the ones that you like the best, and use them on those beliefs. Knock those beliefs down.

Then take action. We live in a world where everything is cocreated, so you have to take action to cocreate the results you want. After that, just take inventory and assess through feedback how you're doing as you go through the steps.

That's what I would do. I'd do it on a regular basis. It could be daily, it could be weekly, it might even be useful to create a mastermind, as described in Napoleon Hill's book *Think and Grow Rich*, where he talked about power of masterminds.

You can create a mastermind. You can get people to come together to go through this book, to help you with your results, with your big intention, your big outrageous, audacious goal, and you can support one another in going for it.

It's an exciting time to be alive. We live in the time of magic and miracles. We have so much technology. We have so many resources. We have so many people thinking big and going out of the box and achieving things that it's mind-blowing.

It's your turn next. Use what you've read here, apply it to the results you want, think bigger than ever before, and expect miracles.

About the Author

D r. Joe Vitale is a globally famous author, marketing guru, movie, tv, and radio personality, musician, and one of the top 50 inspirational speakers
in the world.

His many bestselling books include *The Attractor Factor*, *Attract Money Now*, *Zero Limits*, *The Miracle: Six Steps to
Enlightenment*, and *Anything Is Possible*.

He's also recorded numerous bestselling audio programs, from The Missing Secret and The Zero Point to
The Power of Outrageousness Marketing and The Awakening Course.

A popular, leading expert on the law of attraction in
many hit movies, including The Secret, Dr. Vitale dis-

covered the "missing secret" not revealed in the movie. He's been on Larry King Live, Donny Deutsch's "The Big Idea," CNN, CNBC, CBS, ABC, Fox News: Fox & Friends and Extra TV. He's also been featured in *The New York Times* and *Newsweek*.

One of his most recent accomplishments includes being the world's first self-help singer-songwriter as seen in 2012's *Rolling Stone Magazine*. To date, he has released seventeen albums! Several of his songs were recognized and nominated for the Posi Award, regarded as "The Grammys of Positive Music."

Well-known not only as a thinker, but as a healer, clearing people's subconscious minds of limiting beliefs, Dr. Joe Vitale is also an authentic practitioner of modern Ho'oponopono, certified Reiki healer, certified Chi Kung practitioner, certified Clinical Hypnotherapist, certified NLP practitioner, Ordained Minister, and Doctor of Metaphysical Science.

He is a seeker and a learner; once homeless, he has spent the last four decades learning how to master the powers that channel the pure creative energy of life without resistance, and created the Miracles Coaching® and Zero Limits Mastery® programs to help people achieve their life's purpose. He lives in the Austin, Texas area.

His main site is www.MrFire.com.

INDEX

CPSIA information can be obtained
at www.ICGtesting.com
Printed in the USA
JSHW020847180120
3627JS00002B/2